Pathfinder®Guides

Somerset, the Mendips & Wiltshire

Walks

Compiled by
Brian Conduit and Debbie King

Fully revised by Nick Channer
and Sue Viccars

D0317803

Text: Brian Conduit and Debbie King
Revised text for 2010 edition, Sue Viccars
and Nick Channer
Photography: Brian Conduit, Sue Viccars and Nick Channer
Editorial: Ark Creative (UK) Ltd
Design: Ark Creative (UK) Ltd

© Crimson Publishing, a division of Crimson Business Ltd

This product includes mapping data licensed from Ordnance Survey® with the permission of the Controller of Her Majesty's Stationery Office. © Crown Copyright 2010. All rights reserved. Licence number 150002047. Ordnance Survey, the OS symbol and Pathfinder are registered trademarks and Explorer, Landranger and Outdoor Leisure are trademarks of the Ordnance Survey, the national mapping agency of Great Britain.

ISBN: 978-1-85458-529-5

While every care has been taken to ensure the accuracy of the route directions, the publishers cannot accept responsibility for errors or omissions, or for changes in details given. The countryside is not static: hedges and fences can be removed, field boundaries can alter, footpaths can be rerouted and changes in ownership can result in the closure or diversion of some concessionary paths. Also, paths that are easy and pleasant for walking in fine conditions may become slippery, muddy and difficult in wet weather, while stepping stones across rivers and streams may become impassable.

If you find an inaccuracy in either the text or maps, please write to Crimson Publishing at the address below.

First published 1997.
Revised and reprinted 2002, 2003, 2006, 2010.

Printed in Singapore. 6/10

First published in Great Britain 2010 by Crimson Publishing,
a division of:
Crimson Business Ltd,
Westminster House, Kew Road, Richmond, Surrey, TW9 2ND

www.totalwalking.co.uk

All rights reserved. No part of this publication may be reproduced, transmitted in any form or by any means, or stored in a retrieval system without either the prior written permission of the publisher, or in the case of reprographic reproduction a licence issued in accordance with the terms and licences issued by the CLA Ltd.

A catalogue record for this book is available from the British library.

Front cover: Glastonbury Tor
Previous page: View towards Langport from Huish Bridge

Contents

Approximate walk times

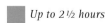 Up to 2½ hours   3–3½ hours   3½ hours and over

The walk times are provided as a guide only and are calculated using an
average walking speed of 2½mph (4km/h), adding one minute for each 10m
(33ft) of ascent, and then rounding the result to the nearest half hour.

SCALE 1:312 500 or 1 INCH to 5 MILES *1CM to 3.1 KM*

0 2 4 6 8 10 KILOMETRES 15
0 2 4 6 MILES 8 10

SPOT HEIGHTS SHOWN IN METRES

PORTISHEAD
Battery Point

BRISTOL

WESTON-SUPER-MARE

NAILSEA
Yatton
Congresbury
Churchill
Axbridge
Cheddar
WELLS
GLASTONBURY
STREET
Wedmore
Woolavington
Somerton
LANGPORT
Ilchester
ILMINSTER
YEOVIL
SHERBORNE

12 3 28 8 22 26 21 24 9 19 5

Keymap 1

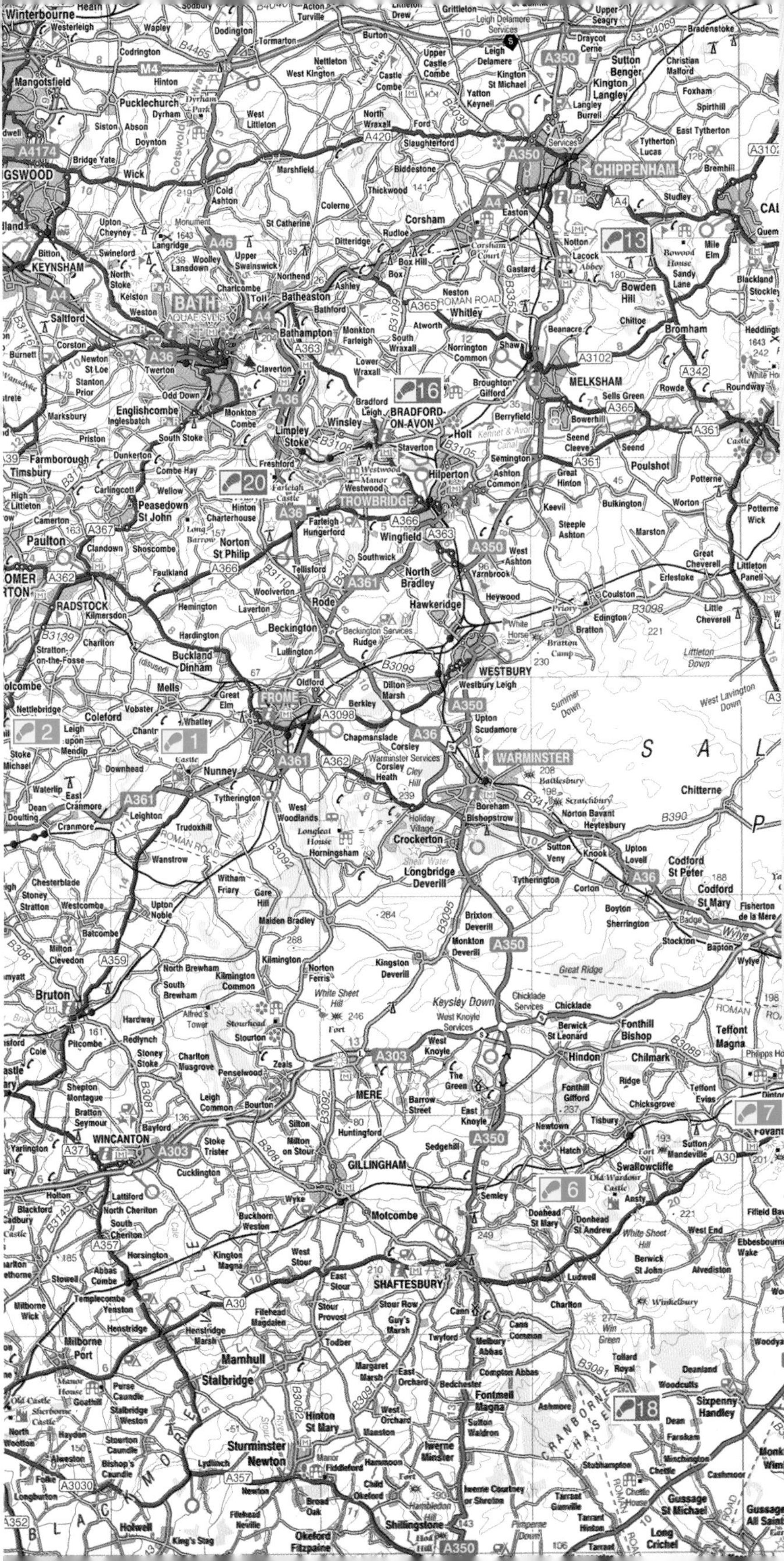

Winterbourne
Mangotsfield
Pucklechurch
Dyrham
Marshfield
Wick
Colerne
Corsham
CHIPPENHAM
Sutton Benger
Kington Langley
Christian Malford
Keynsham
Saltford
BATH
AQUAE SVLIS
Batheaston
Bathampton
Box
Neston
Whitley
Lacock
Bowden Hill
Bromham
MELKSHAM
Bradford-on-Avon
Holt
Winsley
Limpley Stoke
Trowbridge
Hilperton
Semington
Seend
Poulshot
Peasedown St John
Paulton
Timsbury
Midsomer Norton
Radstock
Norton St Philip
Beckington
Rode
North Bradley
Westbury
Edington
Bratton
Frome
Warminster
Coleford
Nunney
Mells
Buckland Dinham
Corsley
Longleat House
Crockerton
Heytesbury
Codford St Peter
Codford St Mary
Chitterne
Bruton
Maiden Bradley
Kilmington
Stourhead
Mere
Zeals
Chicklade
Hindon
Tisbury
Wincanton
Gillingham
Shaftesbury
Motcombe
Semley
Swallowcliffe
Ludwell
Fonthill Bishop
Chilmark
Teffont Magna
Stalbridge
Marnhull
Sturminster Newton
Milborne Port
Templecombe
Shillingstone
Fontmell Magna
Cranborne Chase
Sixpenny Handley
Tollard Royal
Gussage St Michael
Gussage All Saints
Long Crichel
Blackmore Vale
M4
A4
A36
A46
A350
A303
A30
A361
A363
A365
A366
A367
A362
A3098
A357
A371
A3030
A342
A3102
A354
A420
A4174

Keymap 2

SCALE 1:312 500 or 1 INCH to 5 MILES *1CM to 3.1 KM*

0   2   4   6   8   10   KILOMETRES   15

0   2   4   6   MILES   8   10

SPOT HEIGHTS SHOWN IN METRES

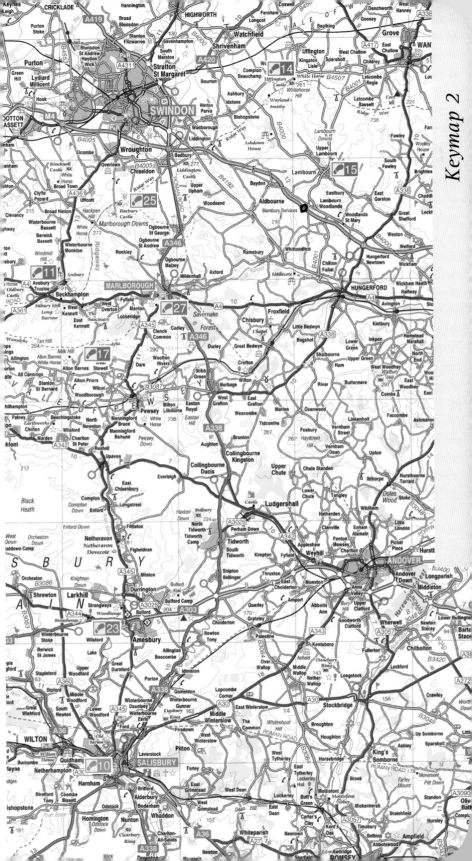

Walk	Page	Start	Nat. Grid Reference	Distance	Time	Height Gain
Avebury, West Kennett and Silbury Hill	35	Avebury	SU 099696	6½ miles (10.5km)	3 hrs	310ft (95m)
Axbridge and Cheddar Reservoir	28	Axbridge	ST 431545	4¾ miles (7.6km)	2½ hrs	n/a
Barbury Castle and Ogbourne St Andrew	77	Barbury Castle Country Park	SU 156760	8½ miles (13.7km)	4 hrs	490ft (150m)
Bradford-on-Avon, Westwood and Avoncliff	48	Bradford-on-Avon	ST 826608	7 miles (11.3km)	3½ hrs	460ft (140m)
Burrington Combe, Dolebury Warren & Black Down	88	Burrington Combe	ST 476588	9¼ miles (14.9km)	5 hrs	1,380ft (420m)
Cadbury Castle and the Corton Ridge	74	Cadbury Castle	ST 632253	7¾ miles (12.5km)	4 hrs	755ft (230m)
Cheddar Gorge	68	Cheddar	ST 461535	6 miles (9.7km)	3½ hrs	1,130ft (345m)
Devizes and Caen Hill Locks	20	Devizes, the Wharf Centre	SU 004617	4 miles (6.4km)	2 hrs	215ft (65m)
Fovant Down	26	Fovant, by the church	ST 996295	4½ miles (7.2km)	2 hrs	475ft (145m)
Glastonbury	64	Glastonbury	ST 498389	7¼ miles (11.7km)	3½ hrs	755ft (230m)
Ham Hill, Montacute and Norton Sub Hamdon	58	Ham Hill Country Park	ST 479168	7 miles (11.3km)	3½ hrs	720ft (220m)
Hinton Charterhouse and Wellow	61	Hinton Charterhouse	ST 771581	7 miles (11.3km)	3½ hrs	755ft (230m)
Ilminster and Herne Hill	22	Ilminster	ST 361145	4 miles (6.4km)	2 hrs	245ft (75m)
Lacock and Bowden Park	40	Lacock, on the edge of the village	ST 918682	6½ miles (10.5km)	3½ hrs	475ft (145m)
Lambourn Downs	46	Lambourn	SU 326789	7 miles (11.3km)	3 hrs	310ft (95m)
Langport and Muchelney Abbey	30	Langport, Cocklemoor car park	ST 419266	5 miles (8km)	2½ hrs	n/a
Leigh Woods and the Avon Gorge	18	Leigh Woods car park	ST 552739	3½ miles (5.6km)	2 hrs	330ft (100m)
Nettlebridge and Harridge Wood	16	Nettlebridge	ST 649486	3½ miles (5.6km)	2 hrs	245ft (75m)
Nunney Combe	14	Nunney	ST 736456	3½ miles (5.6km)	2 hrs	115ft (35m)
Old and New Wardour Castles	24	Old Wardour Castle	ST 938264	4 miles (6.4km)	2 hrs	345ft (105m)
Pewsey Downs	52	Walkers Hill	SU 115638	7 miles (11.3km)	3½ hrs	625ft (190m)
Salisbury and Old Sarum	32	Salisbury	SU 143300	5½ miles (8.9km)	2½ hrs	195ft (60m)
Savernake Forest	84	Marlborough	SU 188692	10 miles (16.1km)	5 hrs	445ft (135m)
Stonehenge	71	Amesbury	SU 149411	8 miles (12.9km)	4 hrs	445ft (135m)
Tollard Royal and Win Green	55	Tollard Royal	ST 944178	7 miles (11.3km)	3½ hrs	675ft (205m)
Uffington Monuments and Vale of the White Horse	43	NT car park on Whitehorse Hill	SU 293866	6½ miles (10.5km)	3 hrs	740ft (225m)
Wells, Ebbor Gorge and Wookey Hole	80	Wells	ST 549457	8½ miles (13.7km)	4½ hrs	970ft (295m)
Weston Woods and Sand Bay	38	Sand Bay car park	ST 328632	6½ miles (10.5km)	3 hrs	560ft (170m)

Comments

A fascinating walk on the Marlborough Downs, taking in the finest collection of prehistoric monuments in the country.

There are views of the Mendips and across the Somerset Levels from this attractive walk that partially encircles Cheddar Reservoir.

From an Iron Age hillfort high up on the Marlborough Downs, the route follows the Ridgeway down into the valley below and then climbs back on to the downs.

There are several hilly sections, but in between much pleasant and relaxing walking by the rivers Avon and Frome and the Kennet and Avon Canal.

The walk leads through woodland and across heathland on to Black Down to reach the highest point on the Mendips. The views from there are superb.

There are magnificent views from both the Corton Ridge and Cadbury Castle, alleged site of King Arthur's court of Camelot.

The final stage of this energetic walk, along the rim of Cheddar Gorge, is particularly spectacular and memorable.

Whether or not you are a canal enthusiast, there is much of interest at the Wharf Centre in Devizes and when descending the Caen Hill flight of locks.

Fovant churchyard and the regimental badges carved on the side of Fovant Down are reminders of the 1914–18 war. There are fine views from the top of the down.

Most of the historic and mythical sites around Glastonbury are linked by this walk, finishing with a climb to the grand viewpoint of Glastonbury Tor.

Chief ingredients of this walk are several grand viewpoints, beautiful woodland, two attractive villages and the chance to visit an Elizabethan mansion.

The walk passes through two villages and there are many fine views over the eastern Mendips.

From the wooded slopes of Herne Hill, there are fine views over Ilminster and the Isle Valley.

An attractive but fairly tortuous route, with superb views over the Avon Valley and the chance to explore a picturesque village and visit an interesting country house.

Enjoy spaciousness and extensive views across the Berkshire Downs on this walk in horse racing country.

An easy but highly atmospheric walk across part of the Somerset Levels and by the River Parrett, with a visit to a ruined abbey.

A walk through attractive woodland is followed by spectacular views of the Avon gorge and Clifton Suspension Bridge.

A secluded valley and quiet woodlands disguise the fact that in Victorian times this was a thriving industrial area.

A beautiful short walk through a wooded combe, with a medieval castle to explore at the end.

You pass through landscaped parkland and woodland on a walk that links a ruined medieval castle with its 18th-century successor.

You enjoy some fine downland walking, grand views over the Vale of Pewsey, two ancient churches and an attractive stretch of the Kennet and Avon Canal.

A fascinating historic walk, much of it beside the River Avon, linking Salisbury with its now deserted predecessor.

Most of this lengthy walk is through the woodlands and along the grand beech-lined avenues of a former royal forest.

The most memorable part of this thoroughly absorbing walk is the approach to Stonehenge across the wide expanses of Salisbury Plain.

There are superb and extensive views both from Win Green, the highest point on Cranborne Chase, and the subsequent ridge top path.

This modest walk not only visits three major prehistoric sites but also includes a picturesque village and magnificent views over the Vale of the White Horse.

A steady climb on to the Mendip plateau is followed by a descent of Ebbor Gorge. You pass the caves at Wookey Hole and there are grand views of Wells Cathedral on the final stretch.

Much of the walk is along a thickly wooded ridge to the north of Weston-super-Mare and there are some splendid sea views.

Introduction to Somerset, the Mendips and Wiltshire

Both scenically and historically Somerset and Wiltshire must rank as two of the most attractive and interesting counties in the country. Landscapes range from the breezy heights of the Mendips to the flat, watery meadows of the Somerset Levels, and from the rolling chalk uplands of the Marlborough Downs to the mudflats and sandy expanses that fringe the Bristol Channel coast. The variety of sites of historic interest is even greater. What other region can rival the boast of Europe's greatest concentration – and most impressive examples – of prehistoric monuments; two of England's loveliest cathedrals and most attractive cathedral cities; one of the most elegant and dramatic of suspension bridges; plus a fair sprinkling of castles, abbeys and stately homes? This region, where history, myth and legend have become inseparably linked, may have seen the beginnings of Christianity in Britain and was the heartland of both Arthur's kingdom and Alfred the Great's Wessex.

This walking guide does not coincide with the exact boundaries of Somerset and Wiltshire. Exmoor and the Quantock Hills in west Somerset are excluded as they are already covered in another title in the series. But as the North Wessex Downs – the collective name for that great swathe of chalk uplands that sweep across Wiltshire – extend eastwards into neighbouring Berkshire and Oxfordshire, two walks have been included just across the borders of those counties.

Somerset means 'summer pastures' and gets its name from the blue lias town of Somerton, once a place of some importance but now a sleepy though attractive backwater. Stretching across the north of the county from the coastal lowlands in the west and descending to the Frome Valley and Wiltshire border in the east are the Mendips, a range of broad-backed limestone hills. Here is a classic carboniferous limestone landscape of crags, rocky outcrops, deep gorges, caves and waterfalls. Every year thousands come to marvel at the spectacular deep gash of Cheddar Gorge and the highly popular caves at its base, but there are others. To the north is Burrington Combe, situated below the highest point on the Mendips on Black Down (1,067ft). To the south-east is the Ebbor Gorge, which many claim to be the most attractive of all, partly because it is the only one that does not have a road running through it.

To the north the Mendips overlook Bristol, Bath and the River Avon, which flows through another world famous gorge at Clifton; here a natural wonder is spanned by a man-made wonder, Brunel's great suspension bridge. To the south they descend abruptly to the beautiful cathedral city of Wells and the lowlands of the Somerset Levels, one of the most atmospheric and distinctive landscapes in the country and still subject to winter flooding. Above the surrounding wetlands rise low hills, such as the Poldens, and a number of islands or moors on which the main settlements grew up; Athelney, Muchelney and above all the legendary Isle of Avalon. Here stands Glastonbury, seat of the largest and richest monastery in medieval England and centre of a myriad of

Ham Hill

ancient myths and legends. Was it here that Joseph of Arimathea founded the first Christian site in the country? Is the Holy Grail buried here? Are the graves by the transepts of the ruined abbey really those of Arthur and Guinevere? These legends drew medieval pilgrims to Glastonbury and still attract a wide mix of tourists today. Brooding over the whole scene is the mysterious, conical-shaped Glastonbury Tor on which the last abbot was hanged in 1539.

As well as legends, the Somerset Levels have rather more tangible associations with great historic events. It was here that Alfred the Great retreated after his defeat by the Danes, where he is alleged to have burned the cakes, and where he signed a treaty with his Danish enemies at Wedmore in 878. Eight centuries later the last battle on English soil was fought here at Sedgemoor in 1685, when James II defeated the Duke of Monmouth's attempt to seize his throne.

Beyond the levels the land rises again towards the Dorset border. This is warm, honey-coloured hamstone country with picturesque villages, attractive market towns and a number of great country houses. Here is another link with the Arthurian legends, the hillfort of Cadbury Castle, claimed as the site of the king's court of Camelot.

Eastwards is Wiltshire, a county which, like Somerset, takes its name from a once major town – Wilton – that has declined and been superseded by others. The fringes of the Cotswolds clip the north-west of the county and to the east and south of the hills, in the valley of the Bristol Avon, are lovely limestone towns and villages, like Bradford-on-Avon and the National Trust village of Lacock, made wealthy by the profits of the medieval wool trade.

Beyond the Avon lie the great expanses of rolling chalk downs that dominate the landscape of much of Wiltshire. On the Marlborough Downs is the greatest concentration of prehistoric remains in the country, particularly around the great stone circle at Avebury where the West Kennett Long Barrow and Silbury Hill, the highest artificial mound in Europe, are among the sites within easy reach. The downs extend across the Berkshire and Oxfordshire borders to continue as the Berkshire Downs. Here another great prehistoric concentration is centred on the White Horse of Uffington. Traversing the ridge of these downs and linking many of the sites is the Ridgeway, one of the oldest routeways in Europe which is now put to good use as a National Trail.

To the south the Marlborough Downs descend to the beautiful Vale of Pewsey, through which runs the Kennet and Avon Canal, a newer routeway across the region, built in the early 19th century to provide a waterway link between London and Bristol. Here is the valley of the other River Avon, the Wiltshire or Hampshire Avon, which flows across Salisbury Plain. The plain –

The ruins of Glastonbury Abbey

really a gently rolling plateau – occupies the heart of the county. Here is the most famous prehistoric monument of all – Stonehenge – situated on a low ridge in the centre of the plain, visible for miles around and also surrounded by numerous other ancient sites.

A track runs southwards from Stonehenge to Old Sarum, a deserted medieval city. In 1075 the Normans made it the seat of a bishop and within its walls a castle and cathedral were built. In 1220 it was abandoned after the bishop moved down into

Looking down into Cheddar Gorge

the valley below to found New Sarum – better known as Salisbury – on the banks of the Avon. This was a purpose-built city with a new cathedral, built in less than 40 years, which boasts the tallest spire in Britain.

In the south of Wiltshire, near the Hampshire and Dorset borders, stretch more chalk downs, the West Wiltshire Downs and Cranborne Chase, the latter shared with Dorset. This is a former hunting area and here the valleys that cut into the downs are more wooded. From the highest point on the chase at Win Green (911ft) the views are magnificent and even extend to the Isle of Wight.

There are few other areas in the country where history and the landscape are so closely interwoven as in these two Wessex counties. With such a varied countryside and range of historic sites, plus lovely old towns and idyllic villages, attractive pubs and appealing teashops, walking in Somerset and Wiltshire is a sheer joy. Whether you take to the hills or river valleys, downs or woodlands, coast or lowlands, the area is full of fascinating places to seek out.

This book includes a list of waypoints alongside the description of the walk, so that you can enjoy the full benefits of gps should you wish to. For more information on using your gps, read the *Pathfinder® Guide GPS for Walkers,* by gps teacher and navigation trainer, Clive Thomas (ISBN 978-0-7117-4445-5). For essential information on map reading and basic navigation, read the *Pathfinder® Guide Map Reading Skills* by outdoor writer, Terry Marsh (ISBN 978-0-7117-4978-8). Both titles are available in bookshops or can be ordered online at www.totalwalking.co.uk

Nunney Combe

		GPS waypoints	
Start	Market Place, Nunney	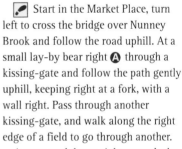 ST 736 456	
Distance	3½ miles (5.6km)	**A** ST 735 457	
Height gain	115 feet (35m)	**B** ST 734 462	
Approximate time	2 hours	**C** ST 736 461	
Parking	Roadside parking in village	**D** ST 742 472	
		E ST 748 469	
Route terrain	Woodland paths, fields and tracks, some muddy after wet weather	**F** ST 737 458	
Dog friendly	On lead through farmland		
Ordnance Survey maps	Landranger 183 (Yeovil & Frome), Explorer 142 (Shepton Mallet & Mendip Hills East)		

This short and easy walk takes you through gently rolling countryside on the eastern slopes of the Mendips. The first half of the route is mostly through the delightful, steep-sided Nunney Combe; the second half is across fields. Muddy conditions can be expected in places.

At Nunney it is the 13th- to 14th-century church, not the castle, that stands on high ground overlooking the attractive village. The reason is that the castle came much later, a small moated tower house, four storeys high, built in the late 14th century by Sir John Delamere. Never very powerful, it succumbed easily to Parliamentary forces after a brief siege in 1645.

Nunney Castle, seen from the churchyard

 Start in the Market Place, turn left to cross the bridge over Nunney Brook and follow the road uphill. At a small lay-by bear right **A** through a kissing-gate and follow the path gently uphill, keeping right at a fork, with a wall right. Pass through another kissing-gate, and walk along the right edge of a field to go through another.

A worn path bears right towards the field edge but the right of way lies straight ahead across the field. In front of a tree-lined embankment **B** turn sharp right downhill across the field. At the bottom keep ahead through a kissing-gate and cross the Nunney Brook **C**. Turn left. Now follows a most attractive part of the walk as you keep beside the brook

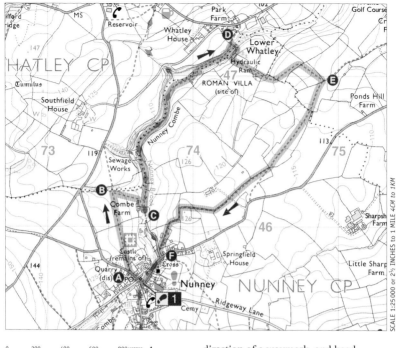

SCALE 1:25000 or 2½ INCHES to 1 MILE 4CM to 1KM

```
0      200     400     600    800 METRES   1
                                            KILOMETRES
                                            MILES
0      200     400     600 YARDS    ½
```

through the wooded, steep-sided Nunney Combe, carpeted with bluebells in spring. On reaching a track, turn left to cross a bridge over the brook. A few yards beyond, turn right to pass a stile, at a public footpath sign, to continue along the opposite bank through the combe. This path is likely to be muddy in places.

The path bears left away from the brook and heads up to a track. Turn right **D** to re-cross the brook and follow the track round a right-hand bend. Where the track bears sharp left, keep ahead, then turn left through a waymarked gate. Continue across a field, keeping close to and parallel with its right edge, and go through a metal gate at the far end. Turn left and keep along the left edge of the next field, by a hedge on the left, in which you need to keep an eye out for a kissing-gate.

Turn left through it, bear right, in the direction of a waymark, and head diagonally across a field to a hedge gap in the far corner. Pass through, keep along the left edge of the next field down to another gap. Turn half-right **E** and head across the next field, making for a kissing-gate. Go through, then another one immediately in front. Turn left along the field edge and shortly afterwards turn right, continuing along the left edge of the field. In the field corner pass to the left of a kissing-gate and bear right to continue along the right edge of the next field. Go through a kissing-gate, cross a track, go through another. Continue along the right edge of the field to pass through a kissing-gate just past a large metal water trough.

Continue along an enclosed, tree-lined path, which, after bearing left and then right through a gate, widens out into a track. Head gently downhill to a lane and turn left down to the main street in Nunney **F**. Turn right, passing the old market cross and **The George pub**, to return to the start. ●

Nettlebridge and Harridge Wood

		GPS waypoints
Start	Nettlebridge	🏁 ST 649 486
Distance	3½ miles (5.6km)	**A** ST 654 484
Height gain	245 feet (75m)	**B** ST 659 482
Approximate time	2 hours	**C** ST 661 480
Parking	Limited laneside parking	**D** ST 656 478
Route terrain	Woodland paths, fields and tracks, some muddy after wet weather	**E** ST 652 479
		F ST 642 478
		G ST 643 483
Dog friendly	Non-dog-friendly stiles, on lead through farmland and Nature Reserve	
Ordnance Survey maps	Landranger 183 (Yeovil & Frome), Explorer 142 (Shepton Mallet & Mendip Hills East)	

The undoubted highlight of this short and easy walk in the eastern Mendips is the middle section which takes you through a beautiful, steep-sided wooded valley along the lower edge of Harridge Wood, passing beside a stream and by rock faces. It is difficult to believe that in the 19th century this peaceful and remote area was the location for a paper mill and housed a busy industrial community. Parts of this route are likely to be muddy after wet weather.

🏁 Begin in the small and scattered hamlet of Nettlebridge. Go through a metal gate just downhill from the post box, at a public footpath sign, and walk along the right edge of a field to a stile. Climb it, bear slightly left across an uneven field, go over a small rise and keep ahead to climb another stile. Continue across a field to a waymarked stile, and on across the next field to where another metal gate leads you on to a lane.

Keep ahead but almost immediately turn right **A** through a metal gate, bear left and walk diagonally across a field, skirting the corner of a wood and eventually bearing right downhill

towards a brook to reach the field end. Climb a stile to rejoin the lane, keep ahead gently uphill, and after ¼ mile turn right **B** down the tarmac drive to Stoke Bottom Farm. Cross a stream, bear left towards the farm, go through the farmyard and turn right **C**, between the house and farm buildings, to a metal gate.

Go through, turn right along the right edge of a field, passing behind the house, and continue by a hedge on the right, bearing left away from the field edge to pass between two old gateposts. To the left is St Dunstan's Well, fed by a small stream, and nearby are several small caves. Continue along the right

Harridge Wood

Now follows a most attractive part of the walk as you continue through a steep-sided, wooded valley – almost a gorge – keeping by a stream on the right, passing limestone rock faces and at one point a waterfall. In spring the wood is carpeted with bluebells. At a three-way fork by a footpath post, take the right-hand uphill path (still in the Oakhill direction), by a wall on the left, which curves right to a stone stile. Climb it and head straight across a field to climb another one in the far left corner just to the right of a bungalow. Turn right **F** along the road, almost immediately turn left over a stone stile, head diagonally across a field and climb another stone stile on to a lane.

edge of a field, by a wire fence and trees on the right, and climb a stile on to a lane **D**. Cross over, bearing right (public footpath sign) through a gate into Harridge Wood Nature Reserve. Head across a field, keeping parallel to the left edge. Later keep alongside the edge of trees and pass through a kissing-gate. Keep ahead to go through another to enter woodland. At a fork and foot-path post to the left of a ruined cottage (now a rare bat habitat) take the left-hand path **E** in the direction of Oakhill.

Turn left and at a crossroads turn right **G** (No Through Road), along very narrow Ash Lane which later descends steeply and rounds a right-hand bend to reach the main road. Turn left with care and after about 100 yds, bear right downhill along an enclosed, tarmac path. The path later widens into a track and passes between houses to reach the starting point by the post box. ●

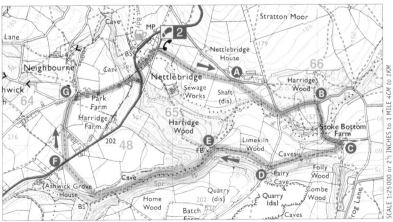

Leigh Woods and the Avon Gorge

		GPS waypoints	
Start	Forestry Commission's Leigh Woods car park, signposted from the A369 to the west of Clifton Suspension Bridge	✍ ST 552 739	
		Ⓐ ST 552 741	
		Ⓑ ST 551 748	
		Ⓒ ST 563 732	
Distance	3½ miles (5.6km)	Ⓓ ST 552 731	
Height gain	330 feet (100m)	Ⓔ ST 551 735	
Approximate time	2 hours		
Parking	Leigh Woods, at start		
Route terrain	Pleasant paths and tracks; steady and prolonged climb through the trees; brief stretch of busy road with pavement		
Dog friendly	On lead through farmland		
Ordnance Survey maps	Landranger 172 (Bristol & Bath), Explorer 154 (Bristol West & Portishead)		

The highlight of this short and easy walk is the middle section along the west side of the Avon Gorge. From here there are dramatic views down the gorge to the Clifton Suspension Bridge. The first and last parts of the route take you through the very attractive Leigh Woods, parts of which form the Avon Gorge Nature Reserve.

River Avon

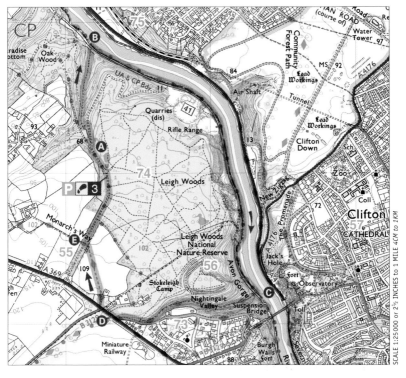

SCALE 1:25 000 or 2½ INCHES to 1 MILE 4CM to 1KM

0 200 400 600 800 METRES 1
0 200 400 600 YARDS ½

KILOMETRES
MILES

🖊 Start by turning left out of the car park and walk gently downhill along a tarmac forest drive, to a fork by a barrier. Keep right here **A**. Follow the broad path and as it curves right, take a path running off sharp left. Follow it downhill through trees and round to the right. Take the next right-hand turning and descend on a stony path to a junction. Keep right and continue through the woods to a disused railway bridge and a T-junction of paths, on the banks of the River Avon **B**.

Turn right to join the Avon Walkway and follow it along the west side of the Avon Gorge – a spectacular walk but also rather a noisy one because of the busy road that runs along the east side. The path, tree-lined at times, keeps below the steep cliffs and later gives grand views of the striking and graceful

Clifton Suspension Bridge, designed by Brunel. Work on the bridge began in 1836 but it was not completed until 1864, five years after Brunel's death.

Just before reaching the bridge turn right **C** at another disused railway bridge to a kissing-gate by a National Trust sign and head steadily uphill through more fine woodland. Eventually the path reaches a kissing-gate on to a road by a National Trust sign for 'Leigh Woods Nature Reserve'. Turn right along the road to a T-junction, then turn right again along the main road to a junction with traffic lights **D**.

Here turn right, at a public footpath sign, along a tarmac track which passes to the right of a bungalow. Climb a stile, and head diagonally across a field towards another bungalow. Turn left at a fence corner to reach a stile, climb it and continue along a track to a tarmac drive. Turn right **E** and follow the drive back to the car park.   ●

Devizes and Caen Hill Locks

Devizes and Caen Hill Locks

Start	Devizes, the Wharf Centre
Distance	4 miles (6.4km)
Height gain	215 feet (65m)
Approximate time	2 hours
Parking	Wharf Centre, Pay and Display car park
Route terrain	Easy towpath and tracks; some reasonably quiet road walking
Ordnance Survey maps	Landranger 173 (Swindon & Devizes), Explorers 156 (Chippenham & Bradford-on-Avon) and 157 (Marlborough & Savernake Forest)

GPS waypoints

◢ SU 004 617
Ⓐ ST 993 615
Ⓑ ST 976 614
Ⓒ ST 979 619

This is essentially a canalside walk and its main feature is the impressive Caen Hill Flight of Locks, one of the major engineering triumphs of the canal age, by which the Kennet and Avon canal descends from the Vale of Pewsey to the Avon Valley. Canal lovers will find much of interest at the Wharf Centre in Devizes and there are fine views over the Avon Valley and downs.

The large, handsome Market Place is the main focal point of Devizes. The town boasts two medieval churches, both dating back to the 12th century; some fine Georgian houses; a Victorian brewery and a 19th-century castle built in the style of its Norman predecessor, on whose site it stands. By the canal, close to the town centre, is the attractively restored Wharf Centre. The two original buildings which survive now house a theatre and the headquarters of the Kennet and Avon Canal Trust – the latter, a former granary, has a shop and museum.

🖉 Facing the canal, turn right under the bridge, then sharp right up to the road and right again to cross the bridge. Turn left to walk along the canal tow-path. Turn left over the first road bridge, left again at a public footpath sign 'Caen Hill Locks via Subway', and then turn sharp left to pass under the bridge.

Continue along the other bank of the canal, passing several locks, go under the next bridge (Prison Bridge) Ⓐ and keep ahead to reach the top of the Caen

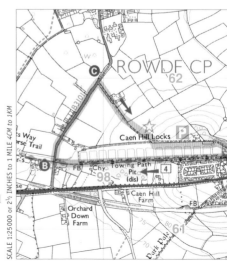

SCALE 1:25000 or 2½ INCHES to 1 MILE 4CM to 1KM

At the top of Caen Hill Locks

Hill Locks. This flight of 29 locks in just over two miles was built by John Rennie, the canal engineer, to overcome the problem of taking the canal up the 237ft rise from the Avon Valley to Devizes. Sixteen of the locks were built close together down Caen Hill, a distance of only about ½ mile.

As you descend gently beside these 16 locks there are fine views ahead over the Avon Valley. At the bottom of the flight go under a bridge **B** and immediately turn left up to a road. Turn sharp left to cross the bridge, continue along the road and at a sign for Caen Hill Locks and the **Lock Cottage Tearooms**, turn right along a tarmac lane **C**.

Follow the lane gently uphill. As it bears left, go right up steps. Turn left along a broad grassy swathe beside the Side Pounds. These square-shaped ponds were built to provide a steady supply of water to the locks. Pass to the right of the parking area; keep ahead on a tarmac path. At the end of the grey metal fencing (right) keep ahead along a tree-lined track, to emerge on to a road. Turn right to cross Prison Bridge, turn left **A** and descend steps, then turn right on to the towpath and retrace your steps to the start.

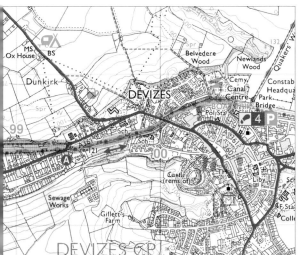

Ilminster and Herne Hill

		GPS waypoints
Start	Market House, Ilminster	✎ ST 361 145
Distance	4 miles (6.4km)	Ⓐ ST 359 143
Height gain	245 feet (75m)	Ⓑ ST 358 139
Approximate time	2 hours	Ⓒ ST 353 139
Parking	Fee-paying signed nearby	Ⓓ ST 337 141
Route terrain	Town roads, woodland paths, fields and tracks, some muddy after wet weather	Ⓔ ST 342 143
Dog friendly	Non-dog-friendly stiles; on lead through farmland	
Ordnance Survey maps	Landranger 193 (Taunton & Lyme Regis), Explorer 128 (Taunton & Blackdown Hills)	

From Ilminster this short walk heads up over the attractive wooded slopes of Herne Hill, then descends into the valley of the River Isle to the village of Donyatt. The return leg takes a more low level route. There are fine views throughout, especially of the town, dominated by the tower of its imposing church.

Ilminster's church, the minster that gives its name to this pleasant and bustling south Somerset market town, is a large and impressive 15th-century building with a tall central tower that can be seen for miles around. The walk starts in the town centre in front of the old Market House.

✎ Walk along Silver Street, in the Langport and Taunton direction, pass to the left of the church and turn left down Wharf Lane. At a T-junction, turn left, then right Ⓐ along Orchard Vale, passing to the left of playing fields.

Head uphill through a new housing

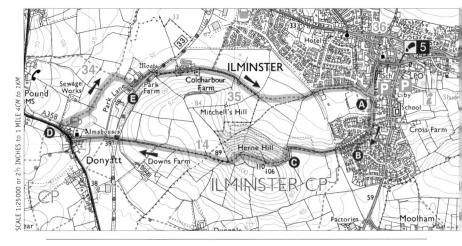

The route offers broad views of Ilminster

area and just where the road curves left near the top, turn right **B** along Herne Rise. Where this ends, keep ahead through a hedge gap and cross a grassy area – the tunnel over the disused Chard Canal, a feeder for the Bridgwater & Taunton Canal (1827) – to reach a junction of tracks. Go through a gate, in the Donyatt direction, and continue along a most attractive enclosed path which curves to the right and gives fine views over Ilminster and the Isle valley. Pass through a gap beside the gate, and follow the path left to continue along the left inside edge of woodland, bearing right **C** to enter Herne Hill Woods.

At a fork immediately ahead take the left-hand upper path, then at the next fork take the left-hand path again, continuing uphill through the trees. At the top, pass to the right of a solitary picnic table and at a crossroads of paths, bear left downhill to a kissing-gate. Go through, here emerging from the woods, and walk along the left edge of a field, keeping ahead at the first corner through a gateway. Ahead are extensive views across the Vale of Taunton towards the Blackdown Hills. Descend gently along the left edge of the next field to cross a stile. Keep ahead along an enclosed downhill path to a lane. Keep ahead towards the picturesque village of Donyatt, crossing

two bridges – the first over a disused railway and the second over the River Isle – then head up to a T-junction to the left of the 15th-century church.

Turn right through the attractive village of warm-coloured hamstone cottages, many of them thatched. After the last of the thatched cottages, turn right **D** along a tarmac track. Ahead are two metal gates: go through the right-hand one and immediately turn half-right to head diagonally across a field. Climb a half-hidden stile and footbridge in the far corner and continue along the curving right-hand edge of the next field, with the river over to the right, to a hedge gap. Go through and walk along the right edge of the next field, then turn right to cross a footbridge over the river.

Walk across the field ahead, cross a footbridge and pass a stile. Keep ahead up the right edge of a grassy area, bearing right to a lane. Turn left **E** along the lane. Follow it over the disused railway track again, through the buildings of Cold Harbour Farm, after which it reverts to a rough track. Where this ends at a metal gate and kissing-gate, go through the gate and bear left diagonally across a field *(if planted and impassable, follow the right field edge)* to a metal kissing-gate in the far corner, hidden in the hedge. Continue along the path ahead, go through two kissing-gates and follow a tarmac path ahead to a road.

Bear right, then after a few yards enter playing fields and continue by a fence along their left-hand edge, parallel to the road on the left. In the corner of the playing fields, past the children's playground, turn left through a metal barrier on to the road **A**, then turn left again and immediately turn right along Wharf Lane to return to Ilminster town centre and the start. ●

Old and New Wardour Castles

Old and New Wardour Castles

Start	Old Wardour Castle, signposted from the A30 to the east of Shaftesbury	
Distance	4 miles (6.4km)	
Height gain	345 feet (105m)	
Approximate time	2 hours	
Parking	Old Wardour Castle	
Route terrain	Pleasant paths, quiet country road, woodland and farmland tracks	
Dog friendly	Non-dog-friendly stiles	
Ordnance Survey maps	Landranger 184 (Salisbury & The Plain), Explorer 118 (Shaftesbury & Cranborne Chase)	

GPS waypoints

🖉 ST 938 264
Ⓐ ST 934 261
Ⓑ ST 927 272
Ⓒ ST 931 276
Ⓓ ST 934 279
Ⓔ ST 941 271
Ⓕ ST 945 263

A ruined medieval castle and its 18th-century successor are linked by this undulating and interesting walk near the northern edge of Cranborne Chase. The route passes through a varied and attractive mixture of landscaped parkland, farmland and woodland. There is some modest climbing on the latter stages and a final descent through woodland.

The ruins of Old Wardour Castle are much enhanced by their romantic setting in landscaped grounds beside a

The medieval ruins of Old Wardour Castle

lake and are well worth a visit. The hexagonal-shaped castle dates from the 14th century, but after its purchase by the Arundell family in 1570 it was partially rebuilt and made more comfortable. After the Civil War it was abandoned and fell into ruin but the landscaping of the grounds in the 18th century led to the building of a 'Gothick' summer house and the construction of a grotto, a popular contemporary feature.

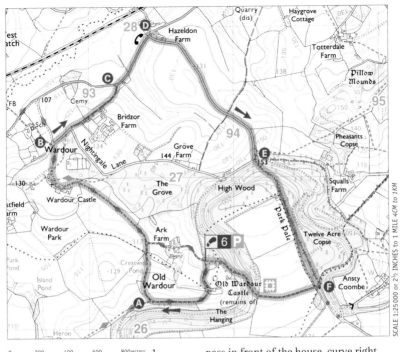

SCALE 1:25 000 or 2½ INCHES to 1 MILE 4CM to 1KM

0	200	400	600	800 METRES	1	KILOMETRES
						MILES
0	200	400	600 YARDS	½		

🖊 Start by taking the tarmac track that leads from the car park, passing between the castle on the left and the lake on the right. After passing to the right of the castle's 18th-century summer house, the track bends to the right and continues as a rough track. Later it becomes enclosed and keeps along the right inside edge of sloping woodland. To the right are grand views across the parkland.

By a waymarked post on the left, turn right **A** on to a clear track that curves left and heads gently downhill between wire fences. When the track bends sharp right, cross a stile on the left and continue towards the imposing bulk of the new Wardour Castle, a grand Georgian mansion built for the Arundells between 1770 and 1776. The house was sold after the Second World War and later used as a girls' school.

Climb a stile and continue ahead to pass in front of the house, curve right and pass between stone gateposts on to a lane **B**. Turn right and where the lane bends right, continue along the tarmac track to Bridzor Farm. Pass to the left of the farm and keep ahead, descending to a road **C**. Turn right, head uphill and at the top – just before a telephone box – turn right along a lane **D**.

Walk gently uphill along this tree-lined lane and keep along it for ¾ mile to where it bears right. At this point keep ahead **E** along a track, entering woodland. The track climbs quite steeply through the trees – at the top continue ahead as the track bends right to a house and continue along a grassy track. This is an area of mixed woodland, a most attractive part of the walk. At a junction of paths and tracks, turn right **F** along a track to emerge from the trees, and at an immediate crossroads keep ahead along an enclosed track across fields. The track then re-enters woodland and descends, passing under an arch, to the start. ●

Fovant Down

		GPS waypoints
Start	Fovant, by the church at the north end of the village	✏ ST 996 295
Distance	4½ miles (7.2km)	Ⓐ ST 998 291
Height gain	475 feet (145m)	Ⓑ SU 002 281
		Ⓒ SU 005 274
Approximate time	2 hours	Ⓓ SU 011 273
Parking	By Fovant church	Ⓔ SU 019 279
Route terrain	Near the start is a section of	Ⓕ SU 006 285
	bridleway which can often be wet and muddy; downland paths and tracks. The last leg is by road through Fovant, back to the start	
Dog friendly	One non-dog-friendly stile	
Ordnance Survey maps	Landranger 184 (Salisbury & The Plain), Explorer 118 (Shaftsbury & Cranborne Chase)	

There are poignant memories of the First World War both at the start of the walk in Fovant churchyard and on Fovant Down, famed for its carvings of regimental badges. After an initial ascent and descent to the west of the village, a steady climb leads on to the crest of the down followed by a walk along the wooded ridge. The views from here are superb. The descent takes you across the face of the down past some of the badges, though these are best viewed from the bottom. The final part of the walk is through the attractive village of Fovant.

At the start of the walk you might like to enter the peaceful and attractive churchyard of Fovant's medieval church. Here are the graves of soldiers from all over the British Empire who died from injuries received during the First World War.

✏ Begin by walking back along the lane to a crossroads, turn left and at a public bridleway sign to the A30, turn right on to a tarmac track Ⓐ. After a few yards this becomes a grassy path, enclosed between hedges and trees, which heads gently uphill through a steep-sided valley to a fork and is often very muddy underfoot.

Continue along the right-hand

enclosed path – this is narrow and likely to be overgrown – which descends gently to reach the A30 to the right of a farm Ⓑ. Cross over and take the lane ahead, signposted to Broad Chalke and Bowerchalke. Where the lane bends right in front of a chalk pit, bear left through a galvanised gate Ⓒ. Continue along the sunken path ahead, climbing steadily up to the ridge of the down, and head up through bushes to reach a gate beyond which is a crossroads Ⓓ. Turn left and walk along a broad, ridge top track through a narrow strip of woodland. Open country can be glimpsed through the gaps in the hedgerow.

Where the track curves right, turn left

over a stile **E** and keep ahead along the right edge of the earthworks of Chiselbury Fort, an Iron Age hill fort which, at a height of 662ft, enjoys a commanding position and magnificent views. Shortly after following the curve of the fort gradually to the left, look out for a footpath sign on a fence on the right and head across.

Follow the path as it runs steeply and diagonally downhill, passing between more of the regimental badges, to the bottom corner of the down. Continue through bushes, keep ahead and go through a metal gate on the right. Walk along the left edge of a field to a metal gate in the corner. At this point look back for a good view of the Fovant Badges, a series of regimental badges

carved on the side of the down by troops stationed here in the First World War.

Go through the gate and turn left along a straight, enclosed track, passing to the left of a large farmhouse. Later the track bears left, then turns right and continues between houses to emerge on to a lane on the edge of Fovant. Keep ahead through the village to the main road **G**, cross over and continue along the lane opposite through this long and strung out village. At a fork in front of the village hall take the left-hand lane, signposted to Tisbury, and at a crossroads turn right along Church Lane to return to the start. ●

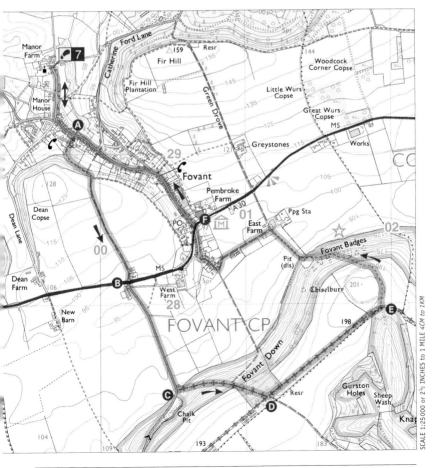

Axbridge and Cheddar Reservoir

		GPS waypoints
Start	Square in Axbridge	
Distance	4¾ miles (7.6km)	ST 431 545
Height gain	Negligible	**A** ST 436 545
		B ST 439 543
Approximate time	2½ hours	**C** ST 448 539
		D ST 450 534
Parking	Two car parks (Pay and Display) signed nearby	**E** ST 427 529
		F ST 425 531
Route terrain	Field paths, level lanes and tracks, pathless riverside meadows	
Dog friendly	Most stiles non-dog-friendly but passable	
Ordnance Survey maps	Landranger 182 (Weston-super-Mare), Explorer 141 (Cheddar Gorge & Mendip Hills West)	

The walk begins by crossing meadows, partially encircles Cheddar Reservoir, continues along enclosed tracks and finishes with a stroll beside two of the waterways of the Somerset Levels. It is a flat walk near the base of the steep Mendip escarpment and provides fine views both of the hills themselves and across the flat, watery expanses of the levels. Some parts are likely to be boggy and waterlogged after wet weather and a couple of paths overgrown but passable; shorts are not recommended in summer.

The square in the centre of Axbridge is a most attractive spot. Just beyond one corner stands the well-proportioned 15th-century cruciform church. In another corner is the picturesque King John's Hunting Lodge – in reality not a medieval lodge at all but the house of a Tudor merchant. It is now a museum.

[✎] Start in the village centre and walk along St Mary's Street, passing the Town Hall. After ⅓ mile turn right **A** down a track (yellow arrow), with a high wall left. This leads to a field; continue along the right-hand edge to cross a stile, then bear left to cross another. Follow the track ahead to reach the reservoir gates **B**.

Keep ahead through a gate (reservoir right) and continue across meadows. Both ahead and to the left are attractive views of the wooded slopes of the Mendips. Go through a gate in a line of trees and keep ahead, by a wire fence bordering trees on the right. Continue past a boatyard – fine views across the reservoir – keeping about 50 yds from the fence, and eventually aiming for a stile in hawthorns ahead. Cross the stile, and follow the path through damp, scrubby woodland (prolific summer vegetation), and continue through trees to cross a stile. Keep ahead to a T-junction of paths.

Turn left, away from the reservoir,

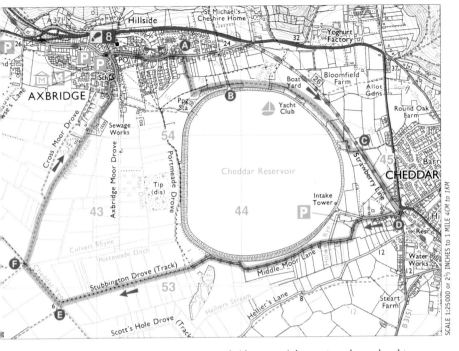

SCALE 1:25000 or 2½ INCHES to 1 MILE 4CM to 1KM

```
0    200   400   600   800 METRES   1
                                        KILOMETRES
                                        MILES
0    200   400   600 YARDS    ½
```

and keep ahead to a gate; turn right **C** along a track. This is part of the Axbridge–Cheddar Cycleway which follows the route of the former Cheddar Valley Railway, nicknamed the 'Strawberry Line'. Over to the left, the gash that can be seen in the line of the Mendips is Cheddar Gorge. In front of a

The Cheddar Yeo River, with the Mendip Hills beyond

bridge turn right up steps, keep ahead to a lane and turn right along it **D**. In front of gates leading to the reservoir, bear left to continue along a pleasant, tree-lined drive, which reduces to a track. When you reach the end of the reservoir follow the track as it bears left. Follow this enclosed track, awash with wild flowers in summer, to reach the Cheddar Yeo River. Cross a footbridge and turn right **E** alongside it. Go through an open gateway, and later a gate; turn right **F** to re-cross the river.

The final part of the walk is very attractive, with views ahead of Axbridge church tower and the Mendips in the background, as you keep straight ahead along the right edge of a field by Ellenge Stream. As the field curves left, keep ahead, over a footbridge and climb a stile. Continue, between a hedge on the left and the stream on the right, climb another stile and keep ahead along a track which continues as a lane into Axbridge. Follow the lane as it bears right, and at a T-junction turn left to return to the village centre. ●

Langport and Muchelney Abbey

		GPS waypoints
Start	Langport, Cocklemoor car park	◢ ST 419 266
Distance	5 miles (8km)	Ⓐ ST 424 263
Height gain	Negligible	Ⓑ ST 418 257
Approximate time	2½ hours	Ⓒ ST 409 248
Parking	Cocklemoor car park (long-stay section, free)	Ⓓ ST 424 248
		Ⓔ ST 428 248
Route terrain	Riverside paths and fields, quiet lanes	
Dog friendly	Dog-friendly gates; on lead through farmland	
Ordnance Survey maps	Landranger 193 (Taunton & Lyme Regis), Explorer 129 (Yeovil & Sherborne)	

This well-waymarked walk, ideal for a languid summer afternoon, is in the heart of the Somerset Levels, a highly distinctive area of low-lying pastures, slow moving rivers and distant views of tall church towers across flat meadows. Much of the route is beside the River Parrett and there is a short detour to the ruins of a medieval abbey. In winter or after rain, some of the riverside meadows may be partially flooded.

Originally an important river port, Langport's prosperity declined with the rise of Bridgwater downstream, but some vestiges of its former greatness remain. On the hill to the east of the town centre is one of the old town gates with the 'Hanging Chapel' above it, and nearby is the 15th-century church.

◢ From the car park, which is signposted from the main street, take the path that leads off from the bottom end, by a rhyne or drainage channel on the left, to the riverbank. Turn left along it, cross a footbridge over the rhyne and follow an embankment above the River Parrett around a slow right-hand curve to Huish Bridge Ⓐ.

Turn right over it, walk along a track, cross a bridge over a rhyne and turn left through a metal gate. After 25 yds (at the end of a wire fence on the right) bear right to descend an embankment, head diagonally across the field and through a metal gate in the far corner. Turn left along an enclosed track; it curves right through another gate. Continue along the right edge of a field by a wire fence and trees. In the field corner, pass through a metal gate and over a rhyne. Keep ahead across the next field, go through a gate, cross the track of the disused railway and go through the gate ahead.

Bear left Ⓑ, walk diagonally across the next two fields, crossing three stiles. Bear right diagonally across the next

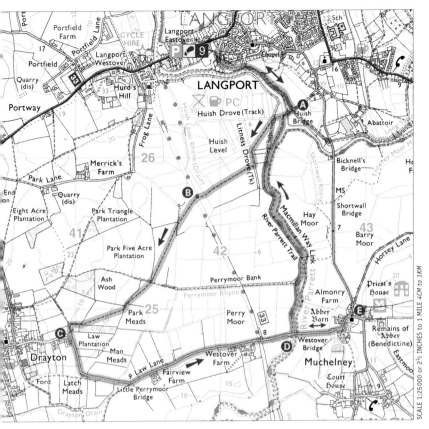

SCALE 1:25000 or 2½ INCHES to 1 MILE 4CM to 1KM

| 0 | 200 | 400 | 600 | 800 METRES | 1 |
| 0 | 200 | 400 | 600 YARDS | ½ | KILOMETRES MILES |

field, bearing left along the hedge at the far end, then turn right through a waymarked gate. Bear left diagonally across the next field and through a gate in the far corner. Continue along an enclosed path and follow it around a left bend to emerge on to a road on the edge of Drayton **C**.

Keep left along the road for just over a mile to Westover Bridge **D**. The route turns left just before the bridge *but keep ahead over it into the village of Muchelney* **E**, *which is well worth a short detour*. Although there is not much left of the abbey except for the foundations, the trio of Benedictine abbey, 15th-century church and 14th-century thatched Priest's House

makes an interesting grouping. The only part of the abbey above ground level is the impressive and largely intact 15th-century Abbot's Lodging.

Return to Westover Bridge **D**, cross it and turn right through a kissing-gate, at a public footpath sign to Huish Bridge. The next part of the walk is along an embankment above the lazily meandering River Parrett, through a series of gates and with extensive views across the meadows. The three church towers that can be seen above the flat terrain are those of Langport, Huish Episcopi and Muchelney.

About 250 yds before Huish Bridge bear right away from the embankment to walk along the riverbank, and climb a stile to reach the track. Turn right, cross Huish Bridge **A** and retrace your steps to the start.

Salisbury and Old Sarum

Start	Salisbury	
Distance	5½ miles (8.9km)	
Height gain	195 feet (60m)	
Approximate time	2½ hours	
Parking	Pay and Display car parks in Salisbury	
Route terrain	Leafy paths, pavements and riverbank	
Ordnance Survey maps	Landranger 184 (Salisbury & The Plain), Explorer 130 (Salisbury & Stonehenge)	

GPS waypoints

- SU 143 300
- Ⓐ SU 141 309
- Ⓑ SU 128 320
- Ⓒ SU 130 325
- Ⓓ SU 133 327
- Ⓔ SU 135 327
- Ⓕ SU 140 326
- Ⓖ SU 135 317

There is considerable historic interest on this walk linking New Sarum (or Salisbury) in the Avon Valley with Old Sarum, its predecessor, on the hill above. The first part of the route follows a delightful stretch of the River Avon to Stratford sub Castle before heading up to the remains of Old Sarum. From this hilltop position you enjoy extensive views over Salisbury, the Avon Valley and Salisbury Plain before descending to rejoin the river. Allow plenty of time to explore both the beautiful cathedral city of Salisbury and the remains of Old Sarum.

The cathedral and city of Salisbury were built on a new site when the seat of the bishop was moved there from Old Sarum in 1220. As a result Salisbury is a rare example of a planned medieval city, laid out on a grid system. Around the spacious Market Place and Guildhall Square, the heart of the city, much of the original street pattern and a number of fine medieval buildings survive.

Standing in a green, walled close – the largest in England – and lined with an assortment of distinguished buildings from the Middle Ages to the 18th century, Salisbury is the only medieval cathedral conceived and completed as a whole. It was built in a remarkably short time, between 1220 and 1258, and therefore has a unique

uniformity of design. Only the upper part of the tower and spire came later, in the early 14th century. The cathedral is a supreme example of the Early English style, with an elaborate west front and lofty nave and choir. In such a spacious setting its beauty can be appreciated from all angles, but the undoubted crowning glory is the graceful, soaring spire, 404ft high, the tallest in the country.

The walk starts at the north-west corner of the Market Place. Cross Minster street into covered Market Walk, following signs to Riverside Walk, cross the River Avon and immediately turn right on to a tarmac path beside it. This is part of the Avon Valley Cycleway. Keep beside the river, passing to the right of car parks and going under several bridges and across roads, to reach a wooden bridge on the edge of parkland **A**.

From here continue along a gravel path beside the river, cross a bridge by a children's play area and immediately turn right to continue along a gravel path.

Take the right-hand – and main – path, rejoining the Avon, and continue along a lovely, tree-lined stretch of the river. Mud can be a problem on these low lying riverside meadows and part of

the route is across boardwalks. Where these end, keep ahead, go through a metal gate. Continue across the meadow and head away from the river. Continue on the path to a stile, turn right along an enclosed path **B**, and cross a bridge over the Avon. Keep ahead, pass beside a metal barrier and continue to a T-junction in Stratford sub Castle. Ahead is a fine view of Old Sarum.

Turn left along a road and just before it bears right by the church – medieval, but with a west tower that was rebuilt in 1711 – turn right on to an enclosed, tarmac path **C**. Follow the path uphill and as it bends to the left, look out for a

SCALE 1:25000 or 2½ INCHES to 1 MILE 4CM to 1KM

The ruins of the former glory of Old Sarum

and some of the walls of the castle, which occupies the centre of the site. As an added bonus the views of the surrounding countryside are superb.

Turn right, go through a small wooden gate ahead, and follow the path downhill. Go through another gate, continue downhill and a few yards before reaching a road, turn right on to a track, at a public footpath sign to Stratford sub Castle. Continue by a hedge along the right edge of a field and halfway across turn left, aiming for a gap in the hedge. Turn right downhill on an enclosed path to eventually pass the Parliament Stone, by a kissing-gate on the right. Near here elections were held for the 'rotten borough' of Old Sarum, so called because, despite having only a handful of voters, it used to elect members to Parliament until such seats were abolished by the Great Reform Act of 1832.

Continue gently downhill and eventually the path broadens out into a track, which leads on to a road. Keep ahead and where the road bends right, turn left through wooden posts **G**, at a public footpath sign to the City Centre, and walk along an enclosed path, between a hedge on the left and a wooden fence bordering a meadow on the right. Later keep ahead along a pleasant, tree-lined, tarmac track and where this ends, with the leisure centre on the right, bear right and cross the wooden bridge over the River Avon **A**, to rejoin the outward route.

Turn left beside the river and retrace your steps to the start. ●

tree-lined path on the right **D**.Continue along this for 100 yds, turn left through a wooden gate, and ascend the hill, eventually bearing left to ascend the steep ramparts. *To explore the castle remains, now managed by English Heritage, take the next path on the right* **E**. Otherwise, continue ahead through a gate and follow this exhilarating stretch along the outer ramparts of the castle. Go through a kissing-gate on to a tarmac drive **F**, which is the main entrance to Old Sarum.

Old Sarum is a fascinating place, for where else can you explore the site of an abandoned medieval city and, at the same time, look down on its successor? As early as the Iron Age a fort was established on this hilltop, but it was after the Norman Conquest that Old Sarum became a thriving city, with the headquarters of the diocese moving here in 1075, and the building of a castle. Several factors led to its decline – the combination of a cramped hilltop position, the lack of a water supply and quarrels between the cathedral and castle caused the bishop to move down the hill in 1220 and found New Sarum or Salisbury. What remains today within the vast earthworks of the outer defences are the bishops' palace, the Norman cathedral and the foundations

Avebury, West Kennett and Silbury Hill

		GPS waypoints
Start	Avebury	
Distance	6½ miles (10.5km)	🖉 SU 099 696
		Ⓐ SU 099 698
Height gain	310 feet (95m)	Ⓑ SU 125 708
Approximate time	3 hours	Ⓒ SU 118 680
Parking	National Trust car park at Avebury	Ⓓ SU 119 674
		Ⓔ SU 114 678
Route terrain	Downland tracks; gently undulating meadow and field paths	Ⓕ SU 104 681
Dog friendly	Some non-dog-friendly stiles	
Ordnance Survey maps	Landranger 173 (Swindon & Devizes), Explorer 157 (Marlborough & Savernake Forest)	

This fascinating walk links the most outstanding collection of prehistoric remains in the country. From the stone circle at Avebury, the route heads up on to the downs and follows a section of the Ridgeway into the village of East Kennett. It then continues to the impressive West Kennett Long Barrow, and the final stretch, mainly by the infant River Kennet, takes you past the intriguing Silbury Hill, the largest artificial mound in Europe. Allow plenty of time in order to appreciate these unique monuments to the full.

A 17th-century antiquarian wrote of the great stone circle at Avebury that 'it did as much excel Stonehenge, as a cathedral does a parish church'. Constructed sometime between 2700 and 1700BC and the focal point of the most important group of prehistoric monuments in the country, it is undeniably impressive, even in an incomplete state. It is also more complex than it seems, with two smaller circles within the main outer ring of stones, and protected by a ditch and embankment. The size of the circle and the proximity of the other monuments suggest that it must have been a major political and/or religious centre of Neolithic Britain.

Partially enclosed by the stone circle, the village of Avebury is a most attractive place in its own right, with an Elizabethan manor house and fine medieval church.

🖉 Begin by taking the tarmac path, signposted Stone Circle, restaurant and shop, that leads from the far corner of the car park. Follow it to a road and turn right Ⓐ through the village, passing through the outer circle. Where the road turns left by the **Red Lion**, keep straight ahead along a lane (Green Street). Pass through the stone circle again and after passing a farm, the lane becomes a rough track which heads steadily uphill on to a ridge.

At a crossroads of tracks turn right on to the Ridgeway **Ⓑ** and follow a track across the downs. The views from here are extensive and wide ranging. Eventually the track descends gently to emerge onto the busy A4 **Ⓒ**. To the left is a group of tumuli and on the other side of the road is the Sanctuary, formerly a double circle of stones linked to Avebury by a stone avenue. Some of the stones that formed this processional avenue survive beside the lane between West Kennett and Avebury.

Walk along the enclosed track opposite, continue downhill between trees, hedgerows and fields and follow it left to a byway sign. Cross a bridge over the River Kennet and continue along a tarmac drive, muddy in places, to a lane. Keep ahead but after a few yards turn right **Ⓓ** at a wall corner along an enclosed path, which leads to a lane. Here turn right through the village of East Kennett and just before the lane crosses the river, turn left along a track.

Pass a left turning and after a few paces turn right at a waymark on a tree

Ⓔ on to a path enclosed by trees. Climb a stile and walk along the left edge of a field, following the field edge as it bears to the left. Climb a stile at the far end, cross a tarmac track and continue along the track ahead. Where it ends, keep along the right edge of a field **Ⓕ** to reach a path on a bend. Here there is a choice.

The route continues to the right but turn left and head gently uphill in order to visit West Kennett Long Barrow. This stone-chambered tomb, dating from around 3700BC, is the largest burial chamber in England, nearly 350ft long. The three huge stones at the entrance were probably placed there when the tomb was sealed up.

As you retrace your steps downhill, the view is dominated by the imposing bulk of Silbury Hill. Follow the path to the left, then pass through a metal kissing-gate and cross a bridge over the river. Keep ahead and go through another metal kissing-gate onto the A4. Turn left and soon after crossing the

The stones of West Kennett Long Barrow

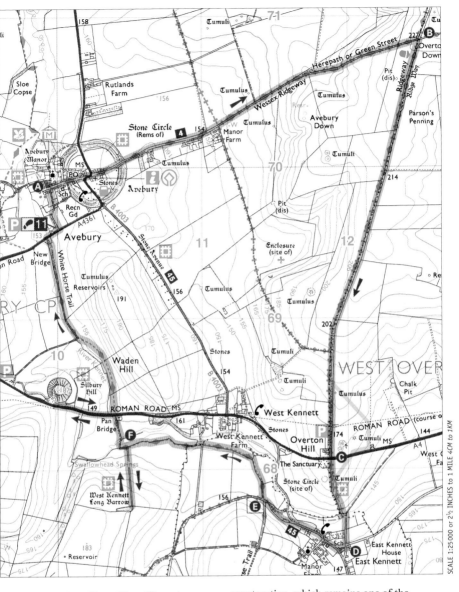

| 0 | 200 | 400 | 600 | 800 METRES | 1 KILOMETRES |
| 0 | 200 | 400 | 600 YARDS | ½ | MILES |

SCALE 1:25000 or 2½ INCHES to 1 MILE 4CM to 1KM

River Kennet again you arrive at Silbury Hill, the largest man-made mound in Europe, 130ft high and covering an area of over five acres. So well built was it that there has hardly been any erosion over a period of nearly 5,000 years. However, investigations and excavations have failed to find out the exact purpose of this incredible feat of construction, which remains one of the great mysteries of prehistory.

Walk back along the road and just after re-crossing the river, go through a wooden gate, to continue along the left edge of a field, by a wire fence and later the river on the left. Go through a wooden gate and follow the Kennet back to Avebury, negotiating a number of stiles and gates. On reaching a road, turn right and almost immediately left into the car park. ●

Weston Woods and Sand Bay

		GPS waypoints	
Start	Sand Bay car park, ½ mile west of Kewstoke village	🏁	ST 328 632
Distance	6½ miles (10.5km)	**A**	ST 331 631
Height gain	560 feet (170m)	**B**	ST 326 627
Approximate time	3 hours	**C**	ST 310 625
Parking	At start	**D**	ST 312 623
		E	ST 337 629
Route terrain	Track through Weston Woods uneven in places; easy lanes and field path; boggy ground after **G**	**F**	ST 336 631
		G	ST 334 636
		H	ST 331 644
Dog friendly	Dog drinking water near water tower between **D** and **E**		
Ordnance Survey maps	Landranger 182 (Weston-super-Mare), Explorer 153 (Weston-super-Mare & Bleadon Hill)		

To the north of the popular resort of Weston-super-Mare the lovely Weston Woods clothe the slopes of Worlebury Hill and give occasional fine views along the length of Sand Bay and across the Bristol Channel to the coast of South Wales. A large proportion of this walk is through these woods, with a brief foray into Weston (as Weston-super-Mare is known locally). The latter part of the route takes you down the medieval Monk's Steps and across fields, with a final section along the shores of Sand Bay.

🏁 From the car park turn right along the road, head uphill to a T-junction and turn right on Kewstoke Road. In front of the **Castle pub** and **wine bar** bear left **A**, at a sign to Weston Woods, on to a track that climbs steadily through the trees. Keep ahead all the while on the main track to reach a crossroads of tracks at the top **B**.

Turn right, passing to the right of radio masts, and continue in a straight line through the woods and eventually the track gently

descends to reach a road by Weston's Old Pier **C**. Walk left along the road, at a fork take the left-hand road, passing

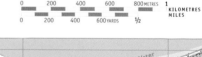

above the pier and gardens, and at the next fork take the left-hand road again (South Road) which curves left.

Opposite a church turn left **D** into Trinity Road and head uphill; then turn sharp right to the road end; take the path ahead to re-enter Weston Woods.

Turn left to climb a flight of steps and at the top turn right along a path that passes through the remains of Worlebury Hillfort, an Iron Age defence. Continue straight ahead along the path as it broadens out into a track, ignoring all side paths and keeping roughly parallel to the outward route. Keep ahead at a signed junction just past the radio masts. Pass a water tower (left), with picnic area right; the track widens and eventually emerges from the woods to continue as a road through a suburban housing area.

At a crossroads in front of Worlebury golf club, turn left **E** along Monks Hill, turn left again into Woodspring Avenue and after 50 yds – by a bench and bus stop – turn right **F** to descend the Monk's Steps, constructed by the monks of nearby Woodspring Priory in the Middle Ages. It is quite a long descent, between trees and with fine views ahead over Sand Bay, *but take care as the steps are uneven and might be slippery*. At the bottom cross a road, turn left and then almost immediately turn right over a stone stile, at a public footpath sign, and descend some more difficult steps. Continue along a path, by a fence on the right, descend a few more steps and go through a squeezer stile on to a road opposite Kewstoke's fine medieval church.

Turn right, take the first turning on the left (Crookes Lane) continue past the **New Inn** and where the road curves left, bear right **G**, at a public footpath sign, along a tarmac drive. After passing to the right of a house, it continues as a narrow, enclosed drive. Go through a metal kissing-gate and continue along the right edge of several low-lying fields, which can be boggy and waterlogged at times, keeping by a hedge on the right and crossing a series of footbridges over ditches. Finally keep along an enclosed, hedge-lined path to a metal kissing-gate, go through and continue to reach a tarmac drive in front of a holiday camp. Where the drive turns left, keep ahead across a grassy area, making for a gap in the far left-hand corner.

Turn left along a drive through a housing development to a road and turn left **H** along the promenade beside Sand Bay to return to the start. On this last leg there are fine views ahead of the wooded headland of Worlebury Hill and to the right across the expanses of the bay to the coast of South Wales. ●

SCALE 1:25 000 or 2½ INCHES to 1 MILE 4CM to 1KM

Lacock and Bowden Park

		GPS waypoints
Start	Lacock	 ST 918 682
Distance	6½ miles (10.5km)	Ⓐ ST 919 691
Height gain	475 feet (145m)	Ⓑ ST 944 702
Approximate time	3½ hours	Ⓒ ST 933 692
Parking	National Trust car park at Lacock	Ⓓ ST 931 683
Route terrain	Deceptively strenuous walk through undulating countryside	Ⓔ ST 924 680
Dog friendly	Cattle-grids; some non-dog-friendly stiles	
Ordnance Survey maps	Landranger 173 (Swindon & Devizes), Explorer 156 (Chippenham & Bradford-on-Avon)	

This is a walk across fields and through woodland in the gentle countryside of the Avon Valley to the north and east of the National Trust village of Lacock. There are some splendid views, especially on the descent through Bowden Park, and a pleasant finale across riverside meadows. Expect some overgrown and muddy paths in places and, as this is a fairly tortuous route, follow the directions carefully.

 Cross the road from the car park and take the path through the trees, signposted 'Village, Abbey Museum and Shops'. At a road, turn left into Lacock. Renowned as one of England's most beautiful villages, Lacock is a harmonious mixture of stone and half-timbered buildings spanning the centuries from the 13th to the 19th. Like many of the nearby Cotswold villages, its wealth and prosperity were based on the medieval wool trade. One of its finest buildings is the mainly 14th- and 15th-century church, unusual in that although cruciform, it has a west tower and spire.

Lacock Abbey was originally an Augustinian monastery, founded in 1232, and when it was converted into a Tudor mansion after its closure in 1539, some of the medieval monastic buildings, including the cloisters and chapter house, were incorporated into the new structure. Further alterations were made in the 18th and 19th centuries. In the middle years of the 19th century it was the home of William Henry Fox Talbot, pioneer of modern photography, and there is a museum commemorating his work near the abbey entrance. Both abbey and village were given to the National Trust in 1944.

Turn right opposite the **Red Lion**, at a T-junction turn right again and in front of the church turn left along a lane, at a No Through Road sign. Cross a footbridge over a brook, by a ford, then at a fork take the right-hand tarmac path to rejoin the lane. Walk uphill to where the lane ends in front of a fence.

Take the path to the right, passing through a kissing-gate, and follow a tarmac path across a field to another kissing-gate on the far side. Go through, continue along an enclosed path to a road, keep ahead for a few yards and turn right to cross the bridge over the River Avon **A**. Turn left over a stile, at a public footpath sign, and walk diagonally across a field, making for a metal stile. Climb it, cross a tarmac drive, climb a metal stile opposite and keep along a narrow, enclosed path. The path curves right, then bends left and you climb two more metal stiles in quick succession before emerging into a field.

Turn left along the field edge, follow it to the right, go across a double stile and then turn right to keep along the top edge of the next field, now with the hedge on the right. Continue to a stile. Climb it and keep ahead along a tarmac path, alongside the partly restored Wilts. and Berks. Canal. To the left is the winding River Avon.

Continue to a bridge, restored by the Wilts. and Berks. Canal Trust and opened by the Duchess of Cornwall in 2009, and keep ahead on the clear path to a stile in the wire fence on the right. Avoid it and take the clear path just beyond it, following it into woodland. Climb out of the trees, cross a stile and go straight ahead across the field. Keep ahead and soon you are alongside trees and boundary hedge on the left. Head towards a house on the skyline, make for a gateway and in the next field turn left to skirt its perimeter, heading for a metal gate on the right of woodland. Go through and continue along the left edge of the next field, cross a track, then bear slightly right away from the field

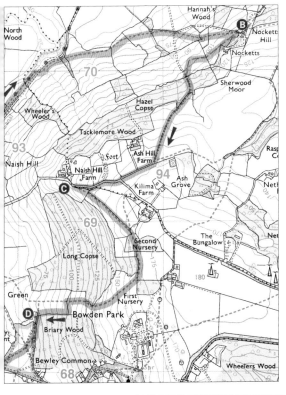

The picturesque village of Lacock

edge and head diagonally uphill to a stile in the far corner.

Climb it and bear right in the field, crossing a stile by a metal gate en route. A few yards in front of a metal gate in the top left corner of the field (with a house beyond) turn sharp right **B** and head back along the top edge of the field just crossed, passing over a double stile/ditch to the right of the field corner. Walk across the next field, bearing left to join a tarmac track running into woodland. Turn left over a cattle-grid, head gently uphill through the wood, emerging from the trees at a cattle-grid.

Continue along the track, at first along the right edge of a field and then heading gently uphill across fields and curving right over a cattle-grid. Go through, continue along the track – now enclosed – to a narrow lane and turn right along it. Follow it as it descends and as it bears right, turn left over a stile **C**. From here there is a grand view over the Avon Valley.

After climbing the stile turn sharp left to keep along the left edge of a field, then bear slightly away from it to go through a metal gate and continue by a wire fence along the left edge of the next field. Climb a stile in the corner to enter woodland, continue through it to a stile. Climb it, keep by woodland and a hedge along the right edge of a field, and just before reaching the field corner, turn right over a waymarked stile.

Head diagonally downhill across Bowden Park – there is a superb view ahead over the Avon Valley with the 18th-century house to the left. Bear gradually right towards the bottom corner of the woodland on the right, and aim for the gap between two belts of woodland. In the bottom right-hand corner of the field, turn right along a track to a stile, climb it, continue downhill across a field and climb another stile beside a gate. Turn left towards woodland, then swing right in front of the trees to keep parallel to them. Make for the woodland corner by a house **D**. Climb a stile and continue along an enclosed track, which continues across open ground. Where it bears left towards a gatehouse, bear right and head diagonally across the open expanse of Bewley Common to a road.

Turn right along it, heading gently downhill all the while, and about 200 yds before reaching the bridge over the river, turn right over a stile **E**, at a public footpath sign, and head across the riverside meadows. To the left Lacock Abbey is glimpsed across the Avon. Bear right towards the hedge on the right edge of the meadow and look out for a footbridge over a ditch and a stile. Climb the stile, keep by a hedge along the left edge of a field, go through a metal gate and bear slightly right across the next field, making for a hedge gap, metal gate and public footpath sign. Climb a stile to the left of the gate and keep ahead by the banks of the placid Avon.

Go through a gate, keep ahead across the meadow – cutting a corner where the river does a loop to the left – and continue to a stile to the right of the bridge. Climb it on to a road, turn left over the bridge **A** and retrace your steps left, bearing left again for the path back to Lacock. ●

Uffington Monuments and Vale of the White Horse

		GPS waypoints
Start	National Trust's Uffington White Horse and Wayland's Smithy car park, on Whitehorse Hill to the south of the B4507	◢ SU 293 866
		Ⓐ SU 301 862
		Ⓑ SU 303 863
Distance	6½ miles (10.5km)	Ⓒ SU 302 872
		Ⓓ SU 304 880
Height gain	740 feet (225m)	Ⓔ SU 293 878
Approximate time	3 hours	Ⓕ SU 289 871
		Ⓖ SU 286 869
Parking	At start	Ⓗ SU 287 856
Route terrain	Downland tracks, minor roads and field paths. There is a steady climb back to the start	Ⓙ SU 281 853
Dog friendly	Some non-dog-friendly stiles	
Ordnance Survey maps	Landranger 174 (Newbury & Wantage), Explorer 170 (Abingdon, Wantage & Vale of White Horse)	

On the slope of the downs, overlooking the Vale of the White Horse and just over the Oxfordshire border, is a group of prehistoric remains that is only eclipsed by the Avebury and Stonehenge complexes. The Uffington Monuments comprise Uffington Castle and the famous White Horse, plus Wayland's Smithy which is about 1½ miles away. From the crest of the downs the route descends into the vale to the village of Woolstone, then climbs back up, and the last part follows a superb stretch of the Ridgeway. As well as the considerable historic interest, the views, both over the downs to the south and the Vale of the White Horse to the north, are magnificent.

◢ At the bottom end of the car park, at a National Trust sign 'White Horse Hill', go through a gate, bear right and follow a worn grassy path across the down. Ahead the outline of the White Horse of Uffington can be seen. Noted for its futuristic design, this is the oldest and best known of all the white horses in England, but the nature of the connection between it and the nearby fort is uncertain.

Cross a lane and keep ahead, at a public bridleway sign, up the slopes of White Horse Hill, keeping ahead at the sign for Uffington Castle. This Iron Age hillfort, which dates from around 500ʙᴄ, stands 856ft above the Vale of the White Horse and is a superb viewpoint.

Follow the path to the triangulation pillar, continue past it to a gate and go through on to the Ridgeway Ⓐ. Turn left and, at a fence corner, turn left over a stile , at a public footpath sign, and walk along by a wire fence on the right-hand edge of a field. As you gently descend, more superb views unfold over the vale. Where the fence turns right, bear right and head across to rejoin it, cutting a corner. The path curves left, passing to the right of the White Horse, and continues down to a lane. Turn right here and follow it downhill with flat-topped Dragon Hill on the left. This natural chalk outcrop, artificially levelled on top, is by tradition the place where St George slew the dragon. Keep on the lane down to the road junction **C**. Cross over and follow the lane ahead towards Faringdon and Uffington. Pass between trees and hedgerows, avoid a footpath to Fawler on the right and continue for a few

paces to a left path signposted Woolstone **D**. Go through the galvanised gate and follow the path ahead between hedgerows and paddocks, then foliage and trees as you head along a green lane. When the track bears left, go straight on at the sign 'Ridgeway Circular Route'. Cut through a wood and then along the left edge of fields to reach the road via a kissing-gate. Keep left through Woolstone, pass a left turning by the **White Horse** **E** and where the lane bends right, keep ahead, at a public footpath sign, along a track to a stile. Climb it, bear slightly right to walk along the left edge of a field, go through a gate, continue along the edge of the next field and climb a

The Vale of the White Horse

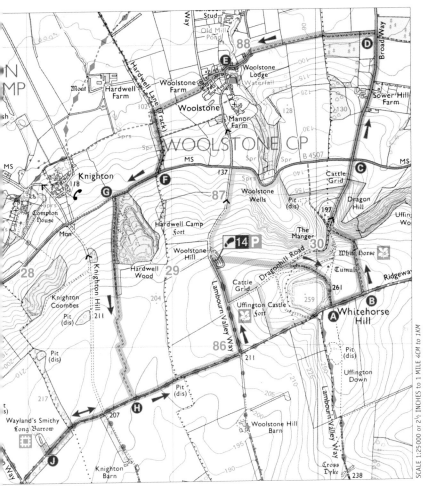

stile to reach a T-junction of paths. Turn left along an enclosed, tree- and hedge-lined path – Hardwell Lane – which ascends gently to emerge on to the B4507 again **F**.

Turn right and while passing the edge of Hardwell Wood, look out for a public footpath sign in the trees and turn left here **G** along a path. Climb up through a wood and continue to emerge into a field. Head straight across it to a fingerpost on the far side where you rejoin the Ridgeway **H**.

Turn right along it to Wayland's Smithy, reached by turning right **J** through a kissing-gate, at a sign for the site and walking along a path. This burial chamber, which lies in a beautiful, secluded spot among trees, was named by the Saxons who thought that it must have been built by one of their gods, Wayland the Smith. In fact it is a Neolithic tomb, built around 3500BC, with a new one constructed on top of it about 200 years later.

Return to the Ridgeway and turn left along it, heading towards White Horse Hill. On reaching a major intersection, turn left for Woolstone, following the Lambourn Valley Way back to the car park where the walk began. ●

Lambourn Downs

Start	Lambourn	**GPS waypoints**	
Distance	7 miles (11.3km)	☑ SU 326 789	
Height gain	310 feet (95m)	Ⓐ SU 319 797	
Approximate time	3 hours	Ⓑ SU 316 803	
Parking	Lambourn	Ⓒ SU 320 811	
Route terrain	Remote downland tracks with little or no shelter from the elements	Ⓓ SU 319 835	
		Ⓔ SU 327 822	
		Ⓕ SU 320 810	
Dog friendly	Expect strings of horses at regular intervals		
Ordnance Survey maps	Landranger 174 (Newbury & Wantage), Explorers 158 (Newbury & Hungerford), 170 (Abingdon, Wantage & Vale of White Horse) and 157 (Marlborough & Savernake Forest)		

There could hardly be a more typical downland walk than this with wide and clear tracks, gentle gradients and expansive views across open, rolling country. Be prepared to share the walk with riders exercising their horses as the Lambourn Downs are very much horse-racing country.

Much of the business and prosperity of the pleasant village of Lambourn revolves around horse racing. The walk starts in the Market Place by the medieval church, an unusually grand building with a fine Norman nave and west front.

☑ Take the paved path to the right of the church, marked by a Lambourn Valley Way footpath sign. The path passes to the left of the brick gatehouse to some picturesque 19th-century almshouses, and emerges via some gate posts on to a road. Keep ahead along this tree-lined road for ¹/₂ mile and where it curves slightly left, at the end of pavement Ⓐ, take a path right, that bears right and runs between fencing and paddocks.

On reaching a lane by the **Malt Shovel**, turn right, then immediately left through Upper Lambourn, passing some

thatched cottages. Where the lane ends, keep ahead along a tarmac path called Fulke Walwyn Way – there is a parallel horse track to the right – and where path and track unite, turn right Ⓑ along a sunken, narrow, tree-lined tarmac track which heads steadily uphill.

Where this track bends sharply right, keep ahead, following Byway and Lambourn Valley Way signs, over a crossroads of tracks and at a fork take the left-hand, hedge-lined track on to the downs Ⓒ. *Note there is a parallel track for horses along here. Avoid it and keep to the narrower path.* At a junction of tracks keep ahead, passing to the right of a Dutch barn, and now come fine, open views across the sweeping, rolling downs as you continue along a gently undulating track.

At a Byway sign merge with a broad track on a bend. About 100 yds before the track curves left – turn right **D** on to a grassy track. Keep ahead along the left-hand track at a fork, skirt the right edge of woodland, pass between wooden barriers and follow the track to a lane. Turn right, follow the lane ahead and round a right-hand bend. At this point a brief detour along the track to the left leads to Seven Barrows, a nature reserve comprising ungrazed chalk grassland in the midst of which are seven Bronze Age barrows, dating from between 1800 and 500BC.

Continue along the lane and where it curves left by Postdown Farm, bear right **E** on to a track that heads steadily uphill over the downs again. The track later narrows to a hedge-lined path where a track joins from the right. Keep ahead, briefly rejoining the outward route, over a crossroads of tracks and at a fork a few yards ahead, take the left-hand track **F**.

At the next fork continue along the right-hand track which heads gently downhill, later keeps along the right inside edge of woodland and becomes a tarmac lane. The lane turns left, then curves right and continues down to a T-junction. Turn left and retrace your steps to the start. ●

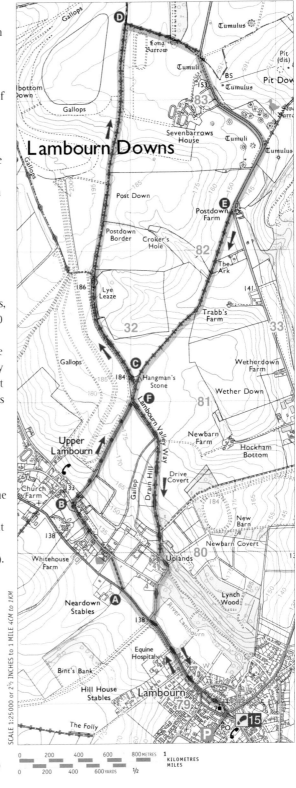

SCALE 1:25 000 or 2½ INCHES to 1 MILE 4CM to 1KM

Bradford-on-Avon, Westwood and Avoncliff

		GPS waypoints
Start	Bradford-on-Avon	✒ ST 826 608
Distance	7 miles (11.3km)	Ⓐ ST 815 603
Height gain	460 feet (140m)	Ⓑ ST 813 598
Approximate time	3½ hours	Ⓒ ST 812 590
Parking	Bradford-on-Avon	Ⓓ ST 811 577
Route terrain	Canal towpath and farmland paths. One steep climb before the walk joins the road near Westwood. Steeply descending field and woodland paths to Avoncliff	Ⓔ ST 803 576
		Ⓕ ST 805 580
		Ⓖ ST 800 592
		Ⓗ ST 804 599
Dog friendly	Some non-dog-friendly stiles	
Ordnance Survey maps	Landrangers 172 (Bristol & Bath) and 173 (Swindon & Devizes), Explorer 156 (Chippenham & Bradford-on-Avon)	

This is a walk of great interest, scenic beauty and variety. It includes attractive waterside stretches along the banks of the rivers Avon and Frome and the Kennet and Avon Canal, farmland, woodland and superb views over both the Frome and Avon valleys. Historic interest is provided by the Saxon church, bridge chapel and tithe barn at Bradford-on-Avon, church and manor at Westwood, ruins of Farleigh Hungerford Castle (which involves a short detour), and the aqueduct at Avoncliff. Some muddy stretches can be expected. Allow plenty of time in order to enjoy this absorbing walk to the full.

Wool is a common link between Bradford-on-Avon and its larger Yorkshire namesake but there the similarity ends. While the northern Bradford expanded into a major industrial city during the Victorian era, Bradford-on-Avon declined, though the imposing 19th-century Abbey Mill would not look out of place in a Pennine valley. The result of this decline is a highly attractive town, sloping steeply down the sides of the valley to the river, with many fine stone buildings belonging to the 16th, 17th and 18th centuries, the heyday of the local Cotswold woollen trade.

The oldest building is the tiny Saxon church, a striking contrast to the imposing medieval church nearby. Built in the 10th century or even earlier, it is one of the best preserved Anglo-Saxon churches in England and was only rediscovered in the 19th century, having been used as a cottage and schoolroom.

The medieval Town Bridge over the Avon has a rare chapel on it, later used as a lock up; the walk starts on the south side of this bridge.

🥾 Walk away from the bridge, passing the War Memorial gardens on the right, and turn right, at a sign for short stay car parking and swimming pool, into a car park. *For a short detour to visit the churches, bear right and cross a footbridge.* Turn left in front of St Margaret's Hall and take the paved riverside path, passing to the right of the Riverside Inn, to follow a pleasant wooded stretch of the Avon.

Pass under a railway bridge and at a T-junction turn right along a tarmac track through Barton Farm Country Park, a thin strip of land between river and canal that extends from Bradford to Avoncliff. Over to the left is the magnificent tithe barn, 168ft long, built in the 14th century to store produce for the nuns of Shaftesbury Abbey. Keep beside the river and after $\frac{1}{2}$ mile, the track bears left (signposted Avoncliff via towpath) uphill to cross a footbridge over the Kennet and Avon Canal Ⓐ. Turn right beside the canal – this path may be muddy – cross a footbridge to a kissing-gate, continue along the right edge of a field and make for a gate in the field corner. Bear slightly left away from the canal and head uphill across the next

The River Avon at Bradford-on-Avon

field towards trees. Do not go through a metal kissing-gate into the trees but turn sharp left and continue along the top edge of the field. From here there is a good view over the town. Continue to a stile, keep going to the next, cross a paddock to the next stile and then continue ahead for a few paces to a stone stile. Follow an enclosed path to the left of a bungalow on to a lane **Ⓑ**.

Cross over, climb a stile and go diagonally across the field with hedge over to the right. About 50 yds before the field corner you reach two stiles on the right; climb the first of these and continue along the left edge of fields, by a hedge on the left, and eventually emerging on to a lane at Westwood. Continue along the lane to a T-junction, cross over, go up steps, through a kissing-gate and walk along an enclosed path. Turn left and follow the path beside a wall into the churchyard, continue through it and go through a metal gate on to a lane **Ⓒ**.

The dominant feature of Westwood's mainly 15th-century church is the tall west tower. To the left is Westwood Manor, also 15th-century but with Tudor and Jacobean additions. It is now owned by the National Trust. Further along the lane to the left is the **New Inn**.

Climb a metal stile opposite, head straight across a field, following the direction of a public footpath sign to Stowford, pass to the left of a circular, tree-fringed pond and go through a gap to continue across the next field. Climb a stile, continue across the next field, go through a metal gate and down the field curving to the right to a gap into the next pasture. Turn immediately left to a second gap, then swing right on to a track, follow it down to a farm and on to a road **Ⓓ**. Turn right, turn left along the drive to Stowford Manor Farm and immediately turn right to head across

grass to a stile. The next part of the route is along a permissive path. Climb the stile and continue across a series of narrow fields, between the road on the right and the River Frome on the left, eventually climbing a stile on to a road to the right of a bridge **Ⓔ**.

The route continues to the right but *turn left uphill if you wish to make a brief detour to visit Farleigh Hungerford Castle.* This was built in the late 14th-century by Sir Thomas Hungerford and was later extended, taking over the entire village in the process. The Hungerfords built a new village and church, with the old church becoming the castle chapel.

On emerging on to the road turn right, not along the main road which curves to the right but along a narrow, uphill lane. Opposite a small lay-by, turn left **Ⓕ** on to a track through trees. Continue along this pleasant, enclosed track from which there are fine views to the left over the Frome Valley. Later the track becomes tree-lined. Continue ahead and eventually reach a stone wall on the left, followed by a lane. Turn sharp right here, climb steeply round to the left and continue on the higher ground. Pass Iford Fields on the right and at the T-junction, turn left along the road by the entrance to **Iford Manor Gardens**, which are open to the public at various times.

After $\frac{1}{4}$ mile turn right **Ⓖ**, at a public bridleway sign to Upper Westwood, along a hedge-lined path to a road. Turn right and after a few yards turn left along a track between houses to a gate. Ahead is a glorious view over the Avon Valley. Go through the gate, head downhill along the right edge of a field and in the field corner turn right through a gate into trees. A few yards ahead turn sharp left, do not go through the gate in front but follow the path to the right and

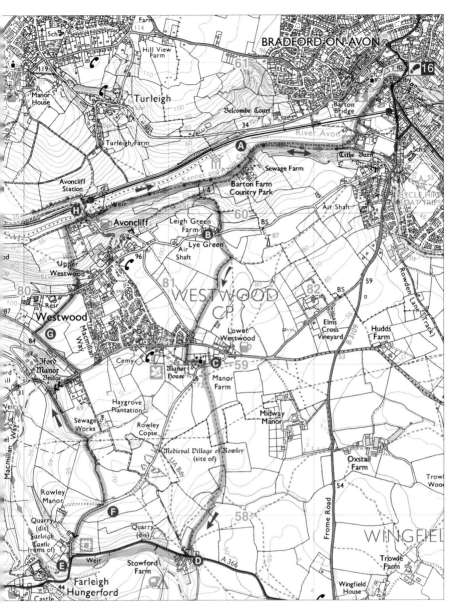

head down to climb a stile into a field. Continue downhill, making for a stile in the bottom right-hand corner, climb it and walk along a track by a wall on the right. Follow the track into Avoncliff and the river is below on the left.

Pass under the Avoncliff Aqueduct, which was built by John Rennie in 1810 to take the canal across the Avon Valley, then head up to the **Cross Guns** and turn sharp right up to the aqueduct **H**. Turn

left, here re-entering Barton Farm Country Park, and follow the quiet, tree-lined towpath back to Bradford-on-Avon.

At the first footbridge **A** you rejoin the outward route – bear left down the tarmac track to the river and retrace your steps to the start. ●

Pewsey Downs

		GPS waypoints
Start	Walkers Hill	
Distance	7 miles (11.3km)	✐ SU 115 638
Height gain	625 feet (190m)	Ⓐ SU 112 629
Approximate time	3½ hours	Ⓑ SU 110 623
Parking	Car park at the top of the hill on the road between Alton Barnes and Lockeridge	Ⓒ SU 105 620
		Ⓓ SU 104 615
		Ⓔ SU 090 620
		Ⓕ SU 095 626
Route terrain	Undulating downland and canal towpath. Approach to Alton Barnes can be overgrown. One steep climb to the Wansdyke	Ⓖ SU 096 635
		Ⓗ SU 101 644
		Ⓙ SU 102 646
Dog friendly	Some non-dog-friendly stiles and turnstiles	
Ordnance Survey maps	Landranger 173 (Swindon & Devizes), Explorer 157 (Marlborough & Savernake Forest)	

The first part of the walk descends from Walkers Hill, high up on the Pewsey Downs overlooking the Vale of Pewsey, and passes through the adjoining hamlets of Alton Priors and Alton Barnes, both with ancient churches, to the Kennet and Avon Canal at Honeystreet. After a walk along the canal, the route continues into Stanton St Bernard and then ascends Milk Hill. On the final exhilarating downland stretch there are more grand views over the vale. The climb back on to the downs is gradual but with one fairly steep section.

✐ From the car park cross the road and go through the gate opposite. Immediately turn left over a stile and walk across the grass, initially by a wire fence bordering the road on the left, later veering slightly right to a stile. Climb it and head diagonally left uphill and over a stile. Keep ahead across the down, passing to the right of Adam's Grave, a prehistoric long barrow which the Saxons called Woden's Barrow, on top of the hill. At the top head south and below you is the outline of the path running down the hillside towards the villages of Alton Priors and Alton Barnes. Make for a gate, here leaving

Pewsey Down Nature Reserve, continue down a path to the road, turn left uphill and after 200 yds, turn sharp right along the White Horse Trail Ⓐ, here a narrow sunken path between trees, running gently downhill between two fields. If overgrown follow parallel field edge. Later continue along a tarmac track to emerge on to a road in the hamlet of Alton Priors. Turn left, immediately turn right Ⓑ along a lane, and where it ends pass through a wooden turnstile – the first of several on the next stage of the walk.

Keep ahead, passing to the right of Alton Priors church. This mainly dates

SCALE 1:25000 or 2½ INCHES to 1 MILE 4CM to 1KM

from the 14th century but the interior is dominated by the fine Norman chancel arch. Continue along a paved path, go through a turnstile, cross two footbridges in quick succession and go through another turnstile. Follow the path over a path junction, head diagonally across a field and go through the last of the turnstiles on to a lane in Alton Barnes. To the left is the tiny

church which is of Saxon origin, restored by the Victorians.

The route continues to the right along the lane to a T-junction **C**. Here turn left along the road into the canal settlement of Honeystreet, which was built in 1811 just after the opening of the Kennet and Avon canal. Remains of the wharf can still be seen. Cross the canal bridge, immediately turn right **D** to descend to the towpath and walk along it, passing the **Barge Inn**. Over to the right the White Horse of Alton

Barnes, which dates from 1812, can be seen on the side of the downs. Pass under the second bridge, immediately turn left up to a track and turn left again **E** to cross the bridge. Follow the track to the left and, in front of Riding School buildings, turn right and then left to reach a lane at a bend. Turn right through the village of Stanton St Bernard, passing to the left of the church – mainly 19th-century except for the medieval tower – and follow the lane around right- and left-hand bends.

After a sharp right bend look out for Coate Road on the left, and turn left by Corner Cottage along it. Follow the lane as it bears left, then right, to meet a T-junction. Turn right along the road. At a public footpath sign and White Horse waymark, turn left **F** and keep straight ahead across huge fields, aiming for the left end of Milk Hill. Cross a track and continue to where the path bends left. Two gates are seen here. Immediately beyond them turn left **G** along the bottom edge of the down, by

The White Horse of Alton Barnes from the canal

a wire fence on the left which gradually curves to the right. Just before reaching the field corner, and a group of hawthorns, bear right and head steadily uphill, by a wire fence on the left. Go through a gap and continue more steeply uphill. Head towards a fence on the skyline and as you approach it, follow the path round to the left. Go through a gate and continue with the fence on the right. Pass through another gate (signs here for the Mid Wilts Way and Whitehorse Trail) **H**. Keep along the fence to the next gate **J**. Turn right and follow a track, soon reaching the edge of a field. Keep left with the Wansdyke on your left. This great earthwork is thought to have been constructed in the 6th or 7th centuries by the Britons as a defence against the invading Anglo-Saxons. Keep along the field edge to a gate in the left bank, leading on to a bridleway. Turn right and follow the track, eventually steadily downhill, by a wire fence on the right, climbing two stiles. Finally go through a gate on to a road and the car park is directly opposite. ●

Tollard Royal and Win Green

		GPS waypoints
Start	Tollard Royal	
Distance	7 miles (11.3km)	🖊 ST 944 178
Height gain	675 feet (205m)	Ⓐ ST 936 187
		Ⓑ ST 929 204
Approximate time	3½ hours	Ⓒ ST 925 206
		Ⓓ ST 937 207
Parking	By village pond at Tollard Royal	Ⓔ ST 948 206
Route terrain	Undulating downland tracks and paths	Ⓕ ST 951 176
Dog friendly	One non-dog-friendly stile	
Ordnance Survey maps	Landranger 184 (Salisbury & The Plain), Explorer 118 (Shaftesbury & Cranborne Chase)	

From the village of Tollard Royal near the Dorset border, several wooded valleys lead up on to a ridge. This route takes one of these, climbing steadily and quite steeply at times, to reach Win Green hill – at 911ft the highest point on Cranborne Chase and a magnificent vantage point. This is followed by a splendid ridge walk, with more outstanding views, and a descent via a parallel valley to return to the start.

Close to the medieval church in Tollard Royal is King John's House – originally a 13th-century hunting lodge, it was remodelled in the 16th century and restored during the Victorian era. Its name indicates that Cranborne Chase, an area of wooded valleys and rolling chalk uplands on the borders of Wiltshire and Dorset, was originally a royal forest – a favourite hunting ground of King John and other medieval monarchs. It became a private chase in the early 17th century when James I bestowed it upon Robert Cecil, Earl of Salisbury.

🖊 Start by taking the tarmac track to the left of the pond and, after a few paces keep left at a fork by some farm outbuildings. The track heads steadily uphill, to a kissing-gate. Go through it and continue by a wire fence on the left

and after going through a metal gate, the track descends. After a few paces turn right through a gate and cross a narrow neck of grass to a further gate. Turn right Ⓐ along a track that continues through Ashcombe Bottom. At a fork, take the left-hand track and follow it as it passes to the right of a cottage.

On the next part of the walk there are two forks in fairly quick succession; in both cases you take the left-hand track, following a series of red-topped metal footpath posts. The track now ascends steeply. At a footpath sign bend left and follow it uphill – here the climb is steep. Pass a private estate sign for oncoming walkers, go through a kissing-gate ahead and head out on to open grassland Ⓑ. Continue uphill, passing a

The ridge path on Win Green hill

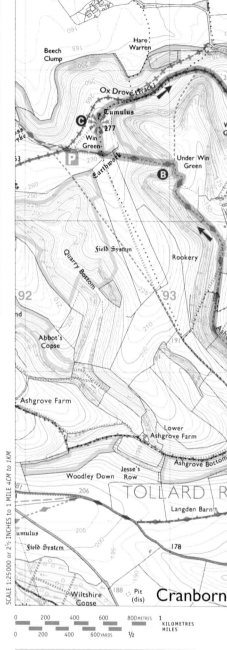

waymarked post, and later bear slightly left to keep alongside a wire fence on the right. Turn right over a stile in that fence and head across to the triangulation pillar and toposcope on the top of Win Green hill, 911ft **C**. From here, the highest point on Cranborne Chase, the magnificent all-round views extend across the wooded slopes of the chase to the Mendips, Marlborough Downs, New Forest, Dorset coast and even the Isle of Wight.

Walk past the triangulation pillar, passing to the left of a tree-encircled tumulus, and bear right around the curve of the tumulus to continue along a grassy downhill track. Bear right on joining a main track – there now follows an exhilarating ridge top walk, with superb views ahead and on both sides. At a junction of tracks bear left, and the track skirts woodland on the right to join a narrow lane **D**. Keep along it for nearly ³⁄₄ mile, still along the ridge top and with conifer woodland

to the right. Opposite a lane to Berwick St John on the left, turn right on to a broad, clear track **E**.

After passing through the narrow belt of conifers, the track descends steadily, enclosed by fences. Where it ends, keep

straight ahead across a large field, making for the right edge of the trees in front. On reaching some gates, turn left for a few paces to a gate and waymark. Go diagonally right in the field towards woodland, continue gently downhill, skirting the right edge of Rotherley Wood, and as you approach the bottom corner follow the field edge to the right.

Descend along a grassy path to another metal gate, go through and continue through Tinkley Bottom, a delightful part of the walk. Go through a metal gate, continue to the point where there is a metal gate on the left and one in front. Turn right **F** and follow a faint path uphill across grass to two gates ahead. Pass through the left-hand one. Walk ahead to a second gate, pass alongside the fence and as you continue over the brow of the hill, the tower of Tollard Royal church edges into view over to the right.

Where the wire fence turns right, continue along the track which heads downhill and then swings to the right. Go through a metal gate on to a road and follow it back to the start. ●

Ham Hill, Montacute and Norton Sub Hamdon

		GPS waypoints
Start	The Prince of Wales pub, Ham Hill Country Park	📌 ST 479 168
Distance	7 miles (11.3km)	Ⓐ ST 491 172
Height gain	720 feet (220m)	Ⓑ ST 491 170
Approximate time	3½ hours	Ⓒ ST 496 169
Parking	Ham Hill Country Park (free parking)	Ⓓ ST 491 163
		Ⓔ ST 486 154
Route terrain	Woodland tracks, field paths, lanes; steep final ascent	Ⓕ ST 471 158
		Ⓖ ST 472 160
Dog friendly	On lead through farmland	Ⓗ ST 479 162
Ordnance Survey maps	Landranger 193 (Taunton & Lyme Regis), Explorer 129 (Yeovil & Sherborne)	

Ham Hill Country Park occupies a ridge that rises to over 300ft and commands superb views over the surrounding countryside. There is an Iron Age hillfort on the site and over the years the land has been extensively quarried. From the starting point you descend through woodland to the village of Montacute, with two brief optional detours. The first of these is a climb to the magnificent viewpoint of St Michael's Hill, and the second is a visit to the 16th-century Montacute House. From Montacute an undulating route leads to the village of Norton Sub Hamdon, and finally comes a fairly steep climb to regain the ridge.

📌 Start in front of the **Prince of Wales** pub and, at a public footpath sign to Montacute, take the path that leads into woodland. At a fence corner a few yards ahead, turn left to descend steps and at the bottom turn right through a gate and continue through the trees. Ignore a footpath sign to East Stoke (left). Follow the sign to Montacute along the left inside edge of Hedgecock Hill Wood. Eventually reach a T-junction of paths at the edge of the wood; bear left downhill, then follow the track right. Where the track turns left, turn right up steps Ⓐ to a gate. Go through and continue along a grassy path as far as the first tree Ⓑ. *At this point turn left for the detour to St Michael's Hill. Head across the grass to a National Trust sign, climb a stile here and bear left to follow a path steeply uphill through trees to the top, crowned by a tower, an 18th-century folly. The magnificent view encompasses Ham Hill, the Somerset Levels, Quantocks, Mendips and Dorset Downs.*

Retrace your steps to point Ⓑ and turn left to rejoin the main route.

SCALE 1:25000 or 2½ INCHES to 1 MILE 4CM to 1KM

Continue along a grassy path, curve left to follow the base of St Michael's Hill and descend gently along the right edge of woodland. At a fork and 'Permissive Path Circular Walk' sign, take the right-hand path and continue gently downhill between tree-lined embankments to a gate. Go through, keep ahead along a tarmac drive, passing the gatehouse of a former Cluniac priory on the right, and go through another gate to a T-junction, where there is a public bridleway sign to Hollow Lane **C**.

The route continues to the right, but *for a brief and very worthwhile detour, turn left and first right into the idyllic village of Montacute,* with its cottages built of the warm brown and honey-coloured hamstone quarried locally, and an attractive medieval church that retains a Norman chancel arch. From The Borough, the handsome square in the village centre, a road leads off to Montacute House, an imposing Elizabethan mansion built between 1588 and 1601. Among its many attractions are a collection of 17th- and 18th-century furniture, Elizabethan and Jacobean portraits and a formal garden and landscaped park. It is now owned by the National Trust.

Retrace your steps to the bridleway sign to Hollow Lane **C** and keep ahead along a stony track, passing to the right of a duck pond. Go through two gates and keep ahead along an ascending track, then go through another gate at the top and turn right uphill along a lane. After a few yards turn right through a kissing-gate and continue up the left edge of a field, soon passing through another. Keep ahead to pass through another gate, and along a wire-fenced path. Pass through two gates to meet a road junction **D**.

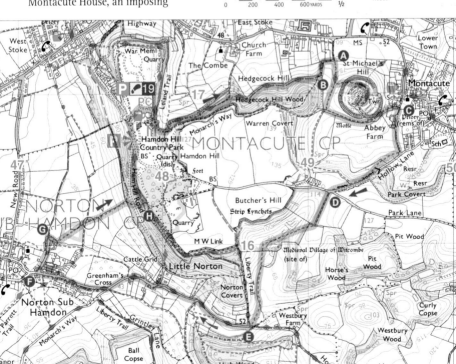

Norton Sub Hamdon

Turn right, and at a public footpath sign to the Witcombe Valley turn left along an enclosed track, which ends at a wooden gate. Pass through, then bear diagonally right downhill – bumps in the field ahead are all that remain of the deserted medieval village of Witcombe – then bear left to follow a grassy path along the bottom of the valley, passing to the right of a clump of trees. Follow the path towards woodland, eventually with a wire fence on the left. The path meets a wooden gate; go through and keep ahead to a tarmac track **E**.

Turn right and follow the narrow track, keeping ahead at a junction, to reach the hamlet of Little Norton. At the T-junction turn left. At the next T-junction, bear right to walk through the picturesque thatched village of Norton Sub Hamdon. The church, built in the late 15th and early 16th centuries, is dominated by its grand 98ft high Perpendicular tower.

Turn right beside the **Lord Nelson F** along Rectory Lane; where the tarmac lane bears right to houses keep ahead (Mill Farm left) along a tarmac track to reach a kissing-gate and public footpath sign on the right. Ahead is the ridge of Ham Hill and its war memorial, and to the left the prominent tower of Norton Sub Hamdon church.

Turn right **G** through the kissing-gate, walk along the right edge of a field, go through a kissing-gate and immediately left through another. Keep ahead to pass through another into Gross's Wood. Follow the path ahead to go through another kissing-gate onto a track.

Turn left, and at a fork a few yards ahead take the right-hand hedge-lined path. Go through two kissing-gates in quick succession, walk uphill along the left edge of a field and go through another kissing-gate in the field corner. Continue uphill through trees, ascend steps to a metal kissing-gate, go through and turn right on to a steeper path. Go up more steps on to a tarmac drive, cross it and continue along the path opposite. Continue steeply up through woodland to a crossroads of paths **H**.

Turn left and walk along a ridge-top path, enjoying superb views. At a fork, take the left-hand path, and continue to a car park. Walk along the left edge and keep ahead on a narrow undulating path, which descends to a road. Turn right opposite the viewpoint parking area; keep ahead to reach a tarmac way, and turn right to return to the start. ●

Hinton Charterhouse and Wellow

		GPS waypoints	
Start	The junction by the Rose and Crown, Hinton Charterhouse		ST 771 581
		A	ST 760 571
Distance	7 miles (11.3km)	**B**	ST 748 568
Height gain	755 feet (230m)	**C**	ST 741 581
Approximate time	3½ hours	**D**	ST 747 582
Parking	Green Lane, Hinton Charterhouse	**E**	ST 757 593
Route terrain	Undulating farmland paths and tracks with several prolonged moderate climbs; quiet country roads	**F**	ST 771 583
Dog friendly	Some non-dog-friendly stiles		
Ordnance Survey maps	Landranger 172 (Bristol & Bath), Explorer 142 (Shepton Mallet & Mendip Hills East)		

The walk starts by folllowing an attractive, undulating circular route between Hinton Charterhouse and Wellow. There are fine views, attractive wooded areas and some pleasant walking beside Wellow Brook. There are also plenty of 'ups and downs' but these are long and steady rather than steep and strenuous. Some of the enclosed tracks and lower level paths may be muddy after wet weather.

Start at a crossroads by the **Rose and Crown**, keep ahead along a lane, signposted as a No Through Road. After passing public footpath signs the path continues downhill and crosses a track at the entrance to farm outbuildings. Continue ahead on the enclosed track and eventually you reach trees. At a fork keep ahead along the left-hand track which turns left into woodland, and at the next fork take the right-hand track. Keep right again at the next fork to continue along a narrow path down to a stile. Go through, turn left along a lane and after 100 yds, turn sharp right **A**, at a byway sign.

Cross a footbridge over Norton Brook

Norton Brook

and follow a track steadily uphill through woodland. Go through a metal gate and keep ahead along an enclosed track, going through gates, to a farm. Pass through the farmyard to the corner of a lane, turn right **B** and continue downhill along this quiet, narrow lane, with fine views ahead of Wellow church and the line of hills beyond. Later descend more steeply and cross a footbridge over Wellow Brook by a ford **C**.

Keep ahead into the village if you wish to visit the **Fox & Badger** *and restored medieval church.* Otherwise turn right over a stile, at a public footpath sign, and continue across meadows, climbing a series of stiles and keeping parallel to the winding brook. Approaching a house at the end of the final meadow, cross a stile and make for a gate leading out to the road.

Turn left and after about 200 yds – on the brow of a hill – turn sharp right at a byway sign **D** along an enclosed path which initially runs parallel to the road. Go through a metal gate and head uphill to the right of a wire fence. Continue ahead as the fence veers to the

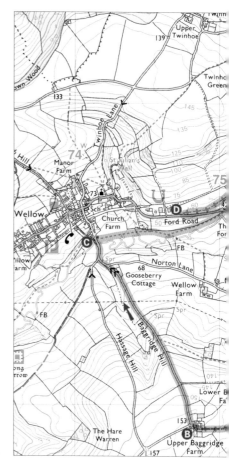

Hinton Charterhouse

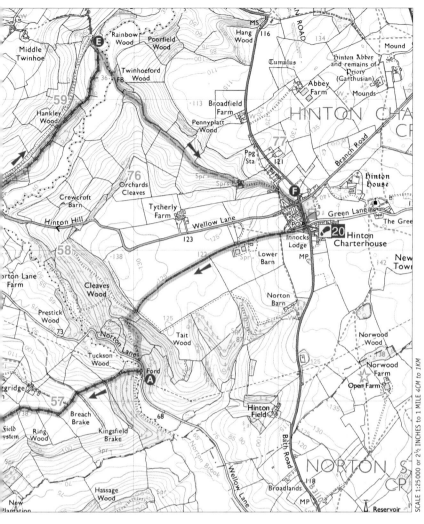

left and after 150 yds bear uphill to a hedge corner. Keep ahead and go through a metal gate in the right-hand corner. Continue through woodland, go through a gate to emerge from the trees and head gently downhill along an enclosed path. In front of two metal gates turn right **E** along the left edge of a field, by Wellow Brook on the left, then turn left to cross two footbridges – the first over the brook itself and the second over another, more minor brook.

Turn right along a path through woodland, recross the minor brook, go through a gate and continue through an attractive narrow valley. Keep along the left edge of a succession of fields and go through a series of gates, ascending gently all the while. Eventually go through a gate in the last field corner on to a track.

Keep ahead between houses and continue uphill along a tarmac track into Hinton Charterhouse **F**. Turn left to the crossroads, then right along the village street to return to the start. ●

Glastonbury

		GPS waypoints	
Start	Market Cross, Glastonbury	☑	ST 498 389
Distance	7¼ miles (11.7km)	Ⓐ	ST 495 388
Height gain	755 feet (230m)	Ⓑ	ST 493 390
Approximate time	3½ hours	Ⓒ	ST 492 391
Parking	Fee-paying nearby	Ⓓ	ST 480 386
		Ⓔ	ST 486 377
Route terrain	Town roads, fields and tracks	Ⓕ	ST 495 383
Dog friendly	Some non-dog-friendly stiles; on	Ⓖ	ST 501 382
	lead through farmland and on	Ⓗ	ST 510 377
	Chalice Hill	Ⓙ	ST 510 388
Ordnance Survey maps	Landranger 182 (Weston-super-Mare), Explorer 141 (Cheddar Gorge & Mendip Hills West)		

Shrouded in mystery and steeped in early Christian and Arthurian legends, the Isle of Avalon around Glastonbury is one of a number of 'islands' that rise above the surrounding marshy and formerly waterlogged 'moors' of the Somerset Levels. This route passes all the well-known sites associated with these legends, beginning with a walk across part of the Levels and along the banks of the River Brue, and continuing over Wearyall and Chalice Hills. A highlight of the walk is the steep climb to the top of the distinctive, conical-shaped Glastonbury Tor, in sight for most of the way and a superb vantage point.

According to legend, St Joseph of Arimathea visited Britain around AD60 and came to Glastonbury. While here he is said to have founded the first Christian church; stuck his staff in the ground on Wearyall Hill, causing it to grow and flower into the Glastonbury Thorn; and hidden the Holy Grail, the cup used by Christ at the Last Supper, beneath a well on Chalice Hill. Later legends linked Glastonbury with the semi-mythical King Arthur, and both he and his wife Guinevere are said to be buried in the abbey, the site of their alleged tomb now marked by a plaque.

If some of the legends are true,

Glastonbury may well be the oldest Christian site in Britain. It is possible that a church was established here in the late Roman period, but the first concrete evidence is the founding of a monastery in the early 7th century. During the Middle Ages this was to become the wealthiest and most powerful in the country, its wealth largely based on its legendary associations. The existing ruins of Glastonbury Abbey are mainly of the church that was rebuilt after a great fire in 1184 and enough survives to give some idea of its size and splendour.

In the town there is further evidence

Glastonbury Tor, seen from the Levels

of the power and influence wielded by the medieval abbots. The 15th-century **George and Pilgrims Inn** probably originated as a guest house for the thousands of pilgrims who came here. The abbot held court in the 15th-century Abbot's Tribunal, now the Tourist Information Centre, and the 14th-century Abbey Barn, now a museum of rural life, used to store the produce brought to the abbey by its many tenants.

From the Market Cross in the town centre walk a few paces along Market Place, then turn right down Benedict Street. Shortly after passing Fairfield Gardens on the left, turn right **A** on to a tarmac track which later becomes an enclosed path to the left of a playing field. Turn left along Bella View Gardens to a T-junction. Turn right towards a road. Cross over and go down a narrow tarmac path. Bear right into Pike Close and at a T-junction take the narrow tarmac path between houses opposite. Turn left towards a road. Turn left along the pavement. Just before the roundabout, cross the road with care and climb a stile, partially concealed behind a laurel hedge **B**. Bear left to pass in front of factory buildings and turn right along a lane. The lane bends left to cross a drainage channel and then bends right to continue alongside it. A few yards on, at a public footpath sign, turn left **C** over a stile and keep along the right bank of a channel (formerly the course of a canal) for the next $3/4$ mile, crossing a footbridge and later a lane (via awkward stiles).

Eventually climb up an embankment above the River Brue. Turn left over a stile, turn right to cross a bridge over the river, and turn left along a road for about $1/2$ mile.

Turn left over the first bridge, turn right through a gate **D** and keep beside the left bank of the Brue, passing through several gates as the river curves left to reach a bridge – the Pons Perilis, or Pomparles Bridge **E**. Climb a stile to meet a busy road, turn right, cross the road at the pedestrian crossing. Turn left, soon turning right into The Roman Way.

Soon after the road curves left and then bends right, look out for some narrow stone steps on the left. Go up them, passing a stone barrier, and bear right to climb steadily over Wearyall Hill, passing through a kissing-gate en route. The view from the top extends across the Somerset Levels to the lines of the Mendips and Quantocks on the horizon; nearer at hand is the Tor, with the town and abbey ruins nestling below it. The alleged thorn which grew here was destroyed by a zealous Puritan in the 17th century but cuttings from it still survive at various sites, including one in the abbey grounds.

Descend to a kissing-gate **F**, and go through to meet a lane, and bear left, later descending to a crossroads. Turn right along Butleigh Road. At the bottom cross Bretenoux Road **G**. Turn left over a stile and walk along the left edge of a field, keeping parallel to the road, eventually passing through a gate. Follow the field edge to the left and right and continue along it, by a hedge on the left. In the field corner turn left over a stile on to a lane **H**, turn left to a T-junction, then turn left again and a few paces farther, turn right over a stile. Head diagonally across a field, aiming for about halfway along the left edge. Climb a double stile, turn right to go through a hedge gap, then cross the stile ahead (or, if easier, go through a hedge gap to the left). Head up to another stile in the left-hand hedge, cross it, then

bear right uphill across a field, making for the far corner, aiming for a hedge gap just left of a house (under telephone wires).

Turn left (busy road) and take the first turning on the right (Well House Lane). Ahead is the Chalice Well, where the water is stained red allegedly because this is where Joseph of Arimathea left the Holy Grail containing the blood of Christ – mineral deposits in the soil may offer a more down-to-earth explanation. Almost immediately after turning into Well House Lane, the route turns right again, at a 'To the Tor' footpath sign, along an enclosed, uphill path which curves left to a kissing-gate.

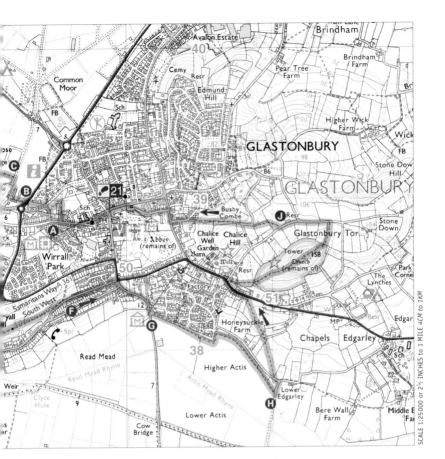

Go through and follow the uphill path ahead – paved in places, with steps and several zigzags – to the tower on the top of Glastonbury Tor. Despite a modest height of only 520ft the climb is quite steep, but the reward is a magnificent view over the surrounding flat country to the Bristol Channel, the Mendips, Quantocks and, in clear conditions, Exmoor and South Wales. The 15th-century tower is all that remains of St Michael's Chapel, where medieval pilgrims used to pray before the last leg of the journey to Glastonbury. In 1539 the last abbot was hanged here for resisting Henry VIII's dissolution of the monasteries.

At the tower turn right, descend steps and follow a concrete path downhill. Go through a kissing-gate at the bottom on to a lane. Turn left, continue downhill, passing a lane (right). At a public footpath post turn right through a kissing-gate **J**. Cross a field, pass through a kissing-gate and continue along an enclosed path to another one. Go through that, turn right along a track to a lane, keep ahead and where the lane bends sharply left, continue along a path. Go through a metal kissing-gate, keep ahead along the top edge of a meadow and descend Chalice Hill to reach a kissing-gate. Go through, keep ahead to a road and walk along it to a T-junction. Turn right and take the first turning on the left (Silver Street). Where the street ends, turn right along a lane into High Street opposite St John's Church and turn left to return to the start.

Cheddar Gorge

Cheddar Gorge

		GPS waypoints	
Start	By the roundabout at the bottom of Cheddar Gorge	☞	ST 461 535
Distance	6 miles (9.7km)	Ⓐ	ST 461 536
Height gain	1,130 feet (345m)	Ⓑ	ST 463 540
		Ⓒ	ST 471 547
Approximate time	3½ hours	Ⓓ	ST 477 557
Parking	Fee-paying, signed nearby	Ⓔ	ST 487 550
Route terrain	Woodland paths, fields and tracks; two long steep ascents, rocky underfoot	Ⓕ	ST 482 545
		Ⓖ	ST 464 537
Dog friendly	Some non-dog-friendly stiles; on lead through farmland and NT land		
Ordnance Survey maps	Landranger 182 (Weston-super-Mare), Explorer 141 (Cheddar Gorge & Mendip Hills West)		

Cheddar Gorge, a 450ft-deep, one-mile-long chasm in the Mendip Hills, is one of the great natural wonders of Britain and this walk enables you to appreciate it at its best. A long, steady and at times steep climb along its north side, much of it through woodland, leads on to the fresh and open expanses of the Mendip plateau. After a descent there is a lovely stretch through a rocky, steep-sided, limestone valley, followed by another climb. Finally comes an exhilarating walk along the south rim of the gorge, with dramatic views down into it – be careful, there are some sheer drops – and extensive views over the Mendips and across the Somerset Levels.

To most people Cheddar is associated with cheese, gorge and caves. Cheese has been made in the area since at least the 12th century. The dramatic scenery of the gorge, coupled with the caves that honeycomb the limestone cliffs, have made the town a popular tourist resort with a multitude of gift shops, cafés, pubs and restaurants. But there is an older Cheddar as well. The Saxon kings of Wessex built a palace here, there is an impressive 14th- to 15th-century church with a tower 110ft high, and an old market cross in the town centre.

☞ The walk begins at the bottom of the gorge at the road junction by Cliff Street car park. Walk along the road towards the gorge, passing the **Riverside Inn & Restaurant** (right), and turn left along The Bays Ⓐ. Where the lane swings right, keep ahead to pass the **White Hart** (left), and at a public footpath sign continue uphill through trees along the side of the gorge, keeping parallel to the road and passing waterfalls.

On rejoining the road by the Cheddar Toy & Model Museum, immediately turn left at a small public footpath sign, on

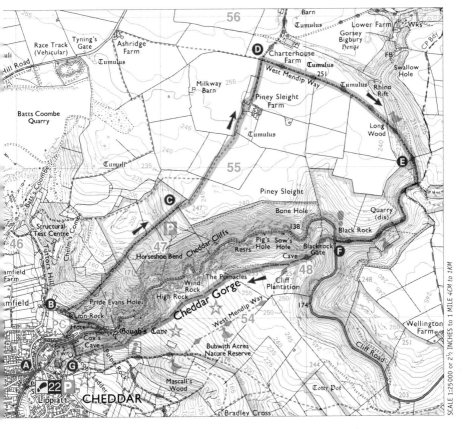

an uphill track. Just after it flattens out, turn right before a house and continue uphill along a narrow, enclosed path. The path bears left and continues up – where it emerges from the enclosed section, to the right of a house, turn sharp right **B**, almost doubling back, on to a steeply ascending path that winds through woodland. Keep ahead, steeply uphill. Eventually pass through a gate and continue uphill, with a wall on the left. At last the path bears left to climb a stile in a wall corner, keep ahead for a few yards and turn right, with the wall on the right again. Continue uphill through a mixture of scrub, gorse and trees and finally climb a stone stile at the top **C**, at a wall corner, to emerge

on to the Mendip plateau. The views over the Mendips and looking back to Cheddar and the reservoir beyond are superb.

Continue along the left edge of a series of fields, negotiating several gates and stiles and keeping parallel to a wall on the left. After climbing a stile, keep along a fenced path to the left of a farm and climb another stile by a tree. Head diagonally right and go through a gate. Turn left along a tarmac track away from the farm buildings. At a public footpath sign by a cattle-grid, turn right **D**, here joining the West Mendip Way, and continue along the right edge of fields. Climb a stile to enter woodland. Descend through the trees and keep ahead through a kissing-gate **E** at the bottom – now comes a particularly attractive part of the walk as you continue through a steep-sided, dry, limestone valley with rocky outcrops, reminiscent of parts of the Yorkshire Dales and Peak District. It is part of the Black Rock Nature Reserve. Later, after the track bends right, the valley becomes more wooded. Continue through it, eventually pass through a gate, then through another to meet a road **F**.

Cross the road and take the steep, rocky uphill path ahead through woodland. Go through a gate at the top, follow the main path and at a fork take the right-hand track, to continue through trees and bracken to a large metal gate. Continue along the path, by a wire fence on the left, to the top of the gorge.

Now comes a succession of spectacular views as you follow a path along the rim of the gorge, with some steep drops on the right, winding steadily downhill through scrub and trees and keeping to the main path all the while. The cliffs lining the gorge are so sheer that the road at the bottom is not visible. Ahead the views extend across Cheddar Reservoir and the Somerset Levels to the coast and Quantocks on the horizon.

Just before reaching Jacob's Tower, opened in 1908, pass through a large metal gate, then turn right **G** down Jacob's Ladder, a long flight of steps – nearly 300 – through woodland that lines the side of the gorge. At the bottom turn left along the road to return to the start.

Cheddar Reservoir and the Somerset Levels make a magnificent backdrop to the Gorge and town

Stonehenge

		GPS waypoints
Start	Amesbury, Recreation Ground car park at the end of Recreation Road just across the bridge over the River Avon	✍ SU 149 411
		Ⓐ SU 144 402
		Ⓑ SU 137 402
		Ⓒ SU 134 399
Distance	8 miles (12.9km)	**Ⓓ** SU 120 413
Height gain	445 feet (135m)	**Ⓔ** SU 120 423
Approximate time	4 hours	**Ⓕ** SU 134 424
		Ⓖ SU 137 428
Parking	Recreation Ground car park at Amesbury	**Ⓗ** SU 152 424
Route terrain	Undulating paths and tracks lead from Amesbury to Stonehenge where the walk joins a National Trust permitted route avoiding main roads	
Ordnance Survey maps	Landranger 184 (Salisbury & The Plain), Explorer 130 (Salisbury & Stonehenge)	

The highlight of this walk is the sudden view of Stonehenge ahead, dominating the skyline of Salisbury Plain and approached on foot across the downs, from where its location can be fully appreciated.

Amesbury is attractively situated on the River Avon which does a great loop to the south-west of the town. The church, with its Norman nave and 13th-century central tower, is unusually imposing. This is because it was probably the church of a medieval nunnery that stood nearby. After the dissolution of the monasteries in the 1530s, a house, Amesbury Abbey, was built on the site, and subsequently rebuilt in the 19th century. It is privately owned and not open to the public.

✍ The walk begins just before the entrance to the Recreation Ground car park. Take the enclosed path which heads down to cross two footbridges, the first one over a stream and the second over the River Avon. Continue along a path which bears right to a crossroads of paths and a footpath post. Keep ahead, in the Durnford direction,

along a steadily ascending, enclosed track. At a crossroads keep ahead over the crest of the hill and then descend gently, with fine views to the right over the Avon Valley, to a dip. Turn right **Ⓐ**, as the track starts to climb and follow the path along the right edge of a field. In the field corner – near a chalk pit on the left – turn left along the bottom edge of the field, keep above a channel on the right, through a wooded area, then turn right over a footbridge. Continue along a winding path through trees – this part of the walk might be overgrown in the summer – and cross a footbridge over the Avon. Keep ahead over a ditch to a kissing-gate. Go through it and follow an enclosed path on to a lane in the hamlet of Normanton **Ⓑ**.

Turn left and just before reaching the medieval church at Wilsford, turn right **Ⓒ** on to the tarmac drive to

Springbottom Farm. After a few yards bear right off the drive and continue steadily uphill along a most attractive, tree-lined path. The path later descends gently and at the bottom bear left to rejoin the drive, which bears left and then curves gradually right, passing to the left of the farm buildings. It then continues as a rough track which peters out just before a fork. Continue along the right-hand, wide, grassy track which heads gently uphill towards the crest of the downs.

On reaching the crest, Stonehenge suddenly appears ahead in the distance, a stunning sight especially as the busy road that runs past it is temporarily hidden from view. Pass between the Normanton Down Barrows, a series of Bronze Age burial chambers that stretches for over $\frac{1}{2}$ mile along the top of this low ridge, and shortly afterwards turn left at a gate **D**. Walk along the edge of a field, go through a gate in the field corner, at a fingerpost turn right along a track to the main A303. Cross over this busy road, keep along the track ahead to the A344 and turn right along it **E**, to the main car park for Stonehenge.

This is the most famous single prehistoric monument in Britain – possibly, indeed, in Europe. Mysteries abound and controversies rage about its purpose and construction, in particular why – and how – the smaller bluestones were brought all the way from the Preseli Hills in Pembrokeshire to be erected here. Although it looks deceptively simple, Stonehenge is a complex monument and appears to have been built in three main phases over a period of around 1,500 years. The first stage was the construction of a large circular bank and ditch around 3000BC. Next, about a thousand years later, came the circles of bluestones, which were subsequently re-arranged. Finally the circle of giant

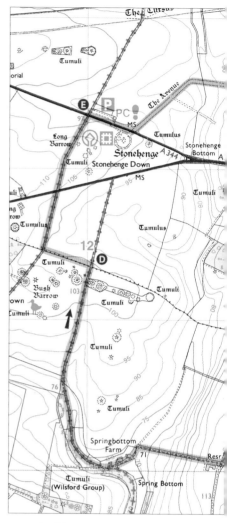

sarsen boulders with lintels, the most striking feature of the monument, was completed around 1400BC. Despite the crowds and the proximity of busy main roads, Stonehenge still manages to exert a powerful influence and one can only marvel at the engineering and organisational skills that were needed for its construction.

In the car park make for the gate with National Trust signs near the main entrance and **refreshment kiosk** and keep right along the field until you are level with the Heel Stone, a single block of sarsen stone, on the opposite side of

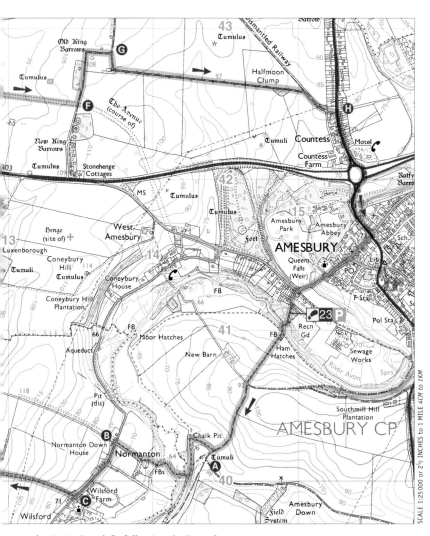

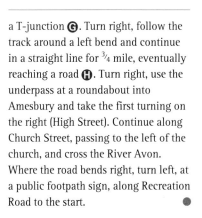

the A344. Bear left, following the line of The Avenue, built and used by early Bronze Age people, probably as a processional route to Stonehenge. The blue stones at the site might have been dragged along The Avenue on the last stage of their journey from Wales. The path's outline is visible, running through the grass. When you see a ladder-stile ahead, make for a gate and fence to the right of it and ascend the hillside, aiming for a gap between two bursts of woodland on the skyline. Head for a gate and turn left along the grassy track **F**.

Shortly after turning right you reach a T-junction **G**. Turn right, follow the track around a left bend and continue in a straight line for ³/₄ mile, eventually reaching a road **H**. Turn right, use the underpass at a roundabout into Amesbury and take the first turning on the right (High Street). Continue along Church Street, passing to the left of the church, and cross the River Avon. Where the road bends right, turn left, at a public footpath sign, along Recreation Road to the start. ●

Cadbury Castle and the Corton Ridge

Start	Cadbury Castle
Distance	7¾ miles (12.5km) including summit of Cadbury Castle
Height gain	755 feet (230m)
Approximate time	4 hours
Parking	Cadbury Castle car park, signed in South Cadbury village
Route terrain	Fields and tracks, open downland and ridges
Dog friendly	On lead through farmland, some non-dog-friendly stiles
Ordnance Survey maps	Landranger 183 (Yeovil & Frome), Explorer 129 (Yeovil & Sherbourne)

GPS waypoints

Start	ST 632 253
A	ST 632 256
B	ST 620 252
C	ST 624 247
D	ST 628 241
E	ST 625 221
F	ST 635 225
G	ST 631 236
H	ST 636 239
J	ST 633 247

From a number of points on the walk there are outstanding views over the surrounding countryside. Foremost among these are Cadbury Castle, alleged site of King Arthur's Camelot; the slopes of Corton Hill; and, especially, the Corton Ridge – a magnificent 1¼ mile ramble. The route passes through three attractive villages and the small amount of climbing involved is steady and relatively easy.

[Start] Turn right out of the car park and turn left up Castle Lane to Cadbury Castle. Go through a gate and continue along an enclosed, uphill track to reach the outer defences of this Iron Age fort.

The site of Arthur's court at Camelot (and, indeed, the very existence of the semi-mythical king himself) is among the greatest and most romantic mysteries of Dark Age Britain, but Cadbury Castle has a better claim than most. Excavations in the 1960s showed that the hill was extensively refortified around AD500, about the time when a great British chieftain – possibly King Arthur – was leading the resistance to the Saxon advance in the south west. Whether or not this is Camelot, the site is an impressive one and the views from it are superb.

Retrace your steps downhill to the lane, turn left through South Cadbury, passing to the right of the medieval church, and at a crossroads in front of the **Red Lion**, turn left **A** along Folly Lane. The lane narrows, becomes an enclosed track and later continues along the right edge of a field, curving gradually left and with Cadbury Castle over to the left all the while.

Look out for where you turn right over a stile by a metal gate on to a narrow lane **B** and turn left along it into Sutton Montis, a small village whose church has a fine 13th-century tower and a Norman chancel arch. Pass the church and at a public footpath sign to Whitcombe and Corton Denham, turn left through a kissing-gate **C**. Walk along the right edge of a field, pass

through a kissing-gate, bear slightly right across an orchard and go through a kissing-gate on to a lane. Go through a metal gate opposite, and bear left along a path to climb a stile. Bear slightly right to walk diagonally up the next field – with a fine view of Corton Hill ahead – and in the far corner climb two stiles in quick succession on to a lane.

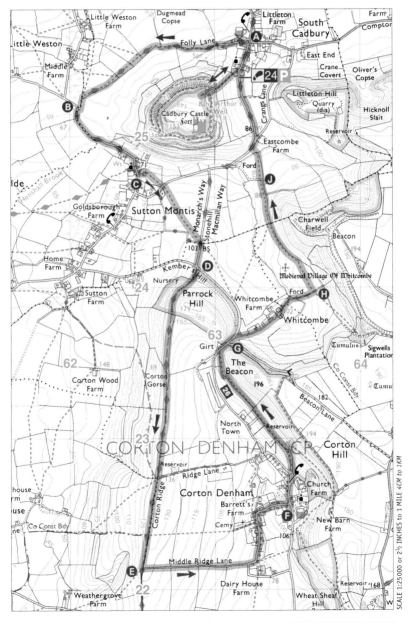

Cadbury Castle, seen from Parrock Hill

Bear right to a T-junction **D**, turn left and then immediately right, at a public bridleway sign to Staffords Green, and continue along an enclosed track to a gate. Go through to emerge on to open grassland, turn right and soon bear left uphill, soon bearing right on a clearer path which continues over Parrock Hill on to the Corton ridge. Now comes the most spectacular part of the walk as you follow a broad, flat, grassy path along the ridge. To the right are extensive views across the lush meadows and fertile farmlands of the Somerset Levels; to the left, in contrast, is the switchback profile of Corton Hill. Pass through a succession of gates, eventually turning left through a metal gate in a field corner, and immediately right through another. Continue along the ridge until you see a wooden seat on the left **E**.

Here turn left through a wooden gate on to a straight enclosed, hedge-lined track – Middle Ridge Lane – which heads steadily downhill to emerge on to a lane. Bear left, following the lane around two bends – first to the left, then to the right – through the village of Corton Denham, then head gently uphill to a T-junction in front of the Victorian church **F**.

Turn left and where the road curves left, bear right, at a public footpath sign to Whitcombe and Corton Hill, along an uphill, sunken, enclosed track. At a fork continue along the left-hand track to a metal gate, go through and keep ahead, slightly above and parallel to the left field edge, to pass a stile. Continue, with a wire fence on the left, contouring along the side of Corton Hill. Where the wire fence ends, descend slightly to continue beneath the bank, with a wire fence left. Just before the field corner, bear left through a gap in a line of trees along a downhill path. After curving right, turn left over a stile and descend steps to a lane opposite a cottage.

Turn right, take the second turning on the right **G**, signposted Whitcombe Farm Lane, and walk along a narrow lane. After passing through a farmyard, the lane continues as a rough track. Bear right to ford a brook and head gently uphill along a tree-lined track to a T-junction of tracks **H**. The bumps in the ground ahead mark the site of the medieval village of Whitcombe (not to be confused with the other medieval village, Witcombe, on the route of Walk 19). Turn left along the right edge of a field, by a wire fence on the right – Cadbury Castle lies immediately ahead – later keeping below an embankment on the right to reach a stile by a metal gate. Cross it and keep ahead, by a line of trees on the right, and in the field corner turn right over a stile and go through a hedge gap on to a track.

Turn left **J** and keep ahead; in the corner of the field cross a footbridge over a brook, and then a stile. Continue across the next field and climb a stile on to a lane. Turn right and follow the lane back to the start. ●

Barbury Castle and Ogbourne St Andrew

		GPS waypoints	
Start	Barbury Castle Country Park, signposted from B4005 to the east of Chiseldon		SU 156 760
		Ⓐ	SU 158 758
Distance	8½ miles (13.7km)	**Ⓑ**	SU 192 746
		Ⓒ	SU 188 722
Height gain	490 feet (150m)	**Ⓓ**	SU 177 728
Approximate time	4 hours	**Ⓔ**	SU 167 731
Parking	Barbury Castle Country Park		
Route terrain	Exposed downland; undulating bridleways and byways		
Ordnance Survey maps	Landranger 173 (Swindon & Devizes), Explorer 157 (Marlborough & Savernake Forest)		

From the superb viewpoint of Barbury Castle, a prehistoric hill fort high up on the Marlborough Downs, the route follows the Ridgeway down into the valley of the little River Og to the village of Ogbourne St Andrew. From here tracks lead back on to the open downs for an invigorating final stretch back to the fort. There are clear, broad tracks all the way, the views are extensive and all the gradients are gradual.

📝 The walk begins on the Ridgeway – possibly the oldest routeway in Britain – which runs along the south side of the car park. *Although the main part of the route lies to the left, first turn right, passing an information centre and going through a gate, to visit the earthworks of Barbury Castle, a large Iron Age fort defended by a double bank and ditches.* The ditches enclose an area of 12½ acres, and the site may have been re-fortified in Saxon times, as excavations have revealed evidence of a long period of occupation. As well as being impressive in its own right, the fort is also a magnificent viewpoint.

Retrace your steps to the car park and continue along the Ridgeway to a gateway. Go through and turn right along a track. At a Ridgeway post turn left **Ⓐ** to follow a track across the downs, keeping along the top of

Marlborough Downs

Smeathe's Ridge. The views from here are superb. Go through a metal gate and after keeping by a wire fence on the right, look out for where the track bears left and downhill away from it.

Go through a gateway at a fork and continue along the left-hand lower track, go through two more metal gates and eventually walk along an enclosed track which descends gently to a lane **B**. Turn right and where the lane bends left, keep ahead along an enclosed, tree-lined track. At a signpost where the enclosed section ends, continue ahead and eventually the tower of Ogbourne St Andrew Church comes into view, nestling at the foot of the down. Eventually the track emerges on to a lane. Turn right along it through the village, passing to the left of the medieval church, to a T-junction.

The **Silks on the Downs,** a gastro pub is off to the left but the route continues to the right **C** along a tarmac drive which soon divides. Stay on the main track and keep ahead, climbing gently back on to the downs. After descending, the track peters out – at this point bear right through a metal gate, head downhill across a field and in the bottom

corner go through another metal gate on to a track **D**. Turn left and the track bends right and heads uphill towards a large barn on the skyline.

Pass to the right of this barn and turn

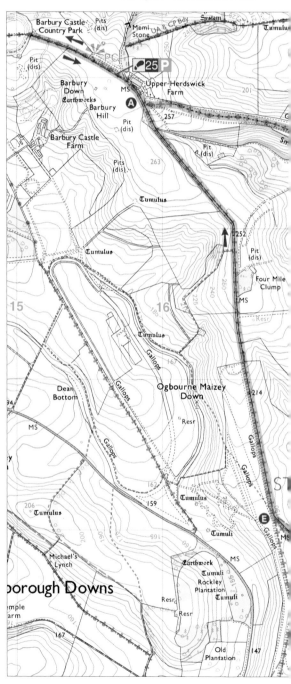

right along a track. On joining a broader track at a Byway sign, bear right along it **E** and follow it gently uphill across the broad downs. The track continues along the left inside edge of a group of trees, Four Mile Clump, and leads back to the start. ●

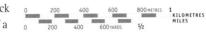

Wells, Ebbor Gorge and Wookey Hole

		GPS waypoints
Start	Market Cross, Wells	
Distance	8½ miles (13.7km)	ST 549 457
Height gain	970 feet (295m)	Ⓐ ST 549 460
Approximate time	4½ hours	Ⓑ ST 542 466
Parking	Wells (fee-paying)	Ⓒ ST 548 471
Route terrain	Field paths and tracks, woodland, lanes; steep ascent up Old Bristol Road to Ⓔ	Ⓓ ST 547 481
		Ⓔ ST 552 488
		Ⓕ ST 535 492
		Ⓖ ST 526 486
Dog friendly	On lead through farmland and Ebbor Gorge National Nature Reserve	Ⓗ ST 528 478
		Ⓙ ST 537 472
Ordnance Survey maps	Landranger 182 (Weston-super-Mare), Explorer 141 (Cheddar Gorge & Mendip Hills West)	

Two of the major characteristics of the Mendip landscape, caves and a gorge, are featured on this walk, along with one of England's most beautiful cathedrals. Much of the route follows the West Mendip Way and the views from the higher points are superb. There is plenty of climbing, especially on the first part in order to get on to the Mendip plateau, and the final stretch gives fine views of Wells Cathedral. Make sure you leave plenty of time to explore the small but fascinating city of Wells.

Situated at the foot of the Mendips, Wells is the perfect English cathedral city. Not only is the cathedral, set in a spacious green close, one of the most beautiful in the country, but the group of ancillary buildings adjoining it are unrivalled. The cathedral mostly dates from the 13th century. Pride of place inevitably goes to the elaborate and striking west front, often considered the best of its kind, but the views of the east end are equally memorable. Inside, attention is drawn to the 14th-century inverted 'scissor' arches – a daring device introduced to support the central tower, which had begun to slip – and

the unique double branching stairs leading to the chapter house. A great favourite with visitors is the clock in the north transept – every hour mounted knights stage a tournament around it.

To the south of the cathedral is the medieval bishop's palace, complete with walls, moat and a drawbridge. Leading off on the north side is the 14th-century Vicar's Close, which claims to be the oldest inhabited medieval street in Europe. It can be reached by a bridge from inside the cathedral.

The walk starts by the Market Cross in the Market Place in the centre of Wells, not far from the cathedral.

SCALE 1:25000 or 2½ INCHES to 1 MILE 4CM to 1 KM

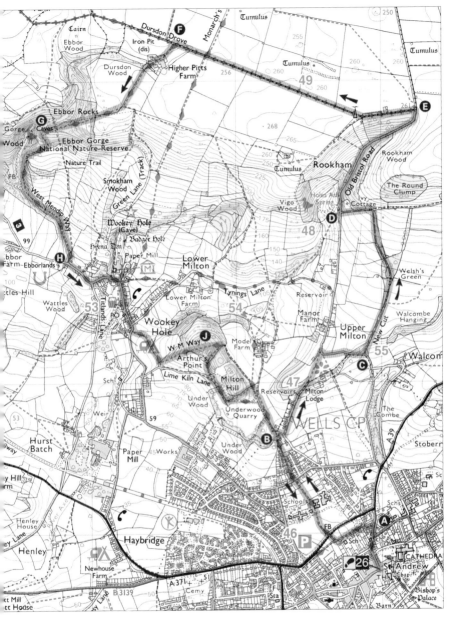

Walk along Sadler Street, passing the **Swan Hotel** on the left, and at a T-junction turn right along New Street. Keep left at a fork, in the 'All Through Routes' direction, and at a West Mendip Way notice, turn left along a tarmac track . Turn first right and then left to continue along Lovers Walk, then keep ahead along a hedge-lined, tarmac path, by school playing fields on the right.

After 250 yds, just before the path bears right, turn right and continue in a straight line over a footbridge and between playing fields and school buildings. Go through a metal gate and

Wells Cathedral

keep along the left edge of a field and head gently uphill, through another gate, to a road. Cross over, take the enclosed tarmac path opposite and slightly left, cross another road, continue uphill, go through a kissing-gate and keep ahead to a lane **B**.

Turn sharp right and take the first turning on the left, Reservoir Lane. The lane continues as a rough track – where this bends left, keep ahead uphill along the right inside edge of woodland and bear right to a stile. Climb it, cross the field (passing to the right of a house) and go through a metal gate in a wall onto a road. Turn right initially uphill, then downhill; where the road curves right, turn left **C**, at a public bridleway sign, along an uphill, enclosed, sunken path. This section may be muddy. The path later winds through woodland to a T-junction. Turn left downhill and continue along a tarmac drive to a road **D**. Turn right, head steeply uphill and at the top turn left along a track, at a Byway sign to Dursdon Drove **E**.

Most of the climbing is now over as you follow this old drove road for just over one mile. Initially tree-lined, it bears right and continues as a wide, straight, enclosed track across the Mendip plateau. At the drive to Higher Pitts Farm turn left **F**, rejoining the West Mendip Way, bear right to pass to the right of the farm and bear left off the track to continue along a path in front of a house. The path bends left to a metal gate. Go through and bear right through the left one of two metal gates, and keep along the right edge of fields, going through another gate and later climbing a stile, which admits you to the Ebbor Gorge National Nature Reserve. Head downhill between gorse and scattered trees, climb a stile, follow the path left and continue downhill through woodland, passing two English Nature car park signs. At the second of these you turn left **G**, but a brief detour ahead brings you to the cliff edge and a magnificent view down the spectacular Ebbor Gorge.

After turning left descend by the side of the gorge, via a winding, stepped path through woodland, to a T-junction. Turn left, later climb a stile to leave the Reserve, and continue along the bottom of the gorge. The track curves right by a cottage to a metal gate. Go through and turn left  along the road through Wookey Hole, passing the entrance to the caves.

At the end of the village turn left through a kissing-gate, at a West Mendip Way sign, head uphill by a hedge along the right edge of a field and go through another kissing-gate. Continue along an enclosed path, go through a kissing-gate and immediately turn left over a wooden stile in a fence. Walk uphill across the next field, skirting the edge of woodland on the left, and continue up to a kissing-gate in the far corner. Follow an uphill track through trees on to the open hilltop, from

which the views are particularly fine, and head for the next group of trees. Here the path bears right and continues steeply downhill through woodland to a kissing-gate. Climb it, continue along a fenced path and go through a gate. Keep ahead along a track, passing limekilns (left), and bear left on joining another, by the huge Underwood Quarry on the right.

Descend to a junction of tracks by a footpath post and turn right along a tarmac drive, still alongside the quarry. At the next West Mendip Way post the drive bears left but you keep ahead along a track, rejoining the outward route. Retrace your steps to the start, enjoying grand views of the cathedral on the descent into Wells.

The Market Place, Wells

Savernake Forest

		GPS waypoints
Start	Marlborough	🏁 SU 188 692
Distance	10 miles (16.1km)	Ⓐ SU 192 694
Height gain	445 feet (135m)	Ⓑ SU 201 694
Approximate time	5 hours	Ⓒ SU 214 697
Parking	Pay and Display car park at Marlborough	Ⓓ SU 214 691
		Ⓔ SU 218 682
		Ⓕ SU 224 679
Route terrain	Forest paths and tracks and a stretch of disused railway	Ⓖ SU 225 668
		Ⓗ SU 208 667
Ordnance Survey maps	Landrangers 173 (Swindon & Devizes) and 174 (Newbury & Wantage), Explorer 157 (Marlborough & Savernake Forest)	Ⓙ SU 208 674
		Ⓚ SU 198 686

The first part of this highly attractive walk is along the Kennet valley to the east of Marlborough, between the Marlborough Downs and Savernake Forest. Most of the remainder is through the extensive woodlands and glades of the forest, survivals of an ancient royal hunting ground that once covered much of eastern Wiltshire. Although a lengthy walk, it is not particularly strenuous and there are no steep gradients, but expect some muddy footpaths in places. There is no right of access in Savernake Forest. However, the public may use it throughout the year, though they are asked to respect the few signs protecting the various groups of private houses on the estate.

Marlborough's long, unusually wide and handsome High Street reflects the town's importance throughout the centuries as a staging post on the main road from London to Bath and Bristol. A church stands at each end of it – at the west end is the 15th-century St Peter's and beyond that the buildings of Marlborough College. At the east end behind the Town Hall is St Mary's, mostly rebuilt in the Cromwellian period following the Great Fire of 1653 which destroyed much of the town and gutted the church, though it does retain a fine Norman doorway at the west end.

🏁 The walk starts at the east end of the High Street in front of the Town Hall, which was built between 1900 and 1902 on the site of its predecessor. Pass to the left of the Town Hall and follow the road to the left, then take the first turning on the right (Silverless Street). Keep ahead at a crossroads by The Green, site of the original Saxon settlement of Marlborough, and continue along the road for 270 yds turning right after a row of houses into Stonebridge Lane Ⓐ. Follow this path downhill and cross the footbridge over the River Kennet. Turn sharp left onto a path and continue as it meanders through fields before veering left at a fork. Cross the river again by a wooden footbridge and turn right to pick up a footpath through the field.

Head across to the right-hand corner of the field and go through a metal gate into woodland, climb a stile, ascend steps, cross a disused railway track **B** and descend steps on the other side. Follow the path along the right edge of a field, and at a corner turn right on to a track. The track soon curves left and continues along the right edge of fields. Go through a kissing-gate just to the left of a field corner, at a public footpath sign and continue along a track between farm buildings. Turn left on to a tarmac drive, immediately turn right and after a few yards turn left up steps and go through a lychgate into Mildenhall (shortened locally to Minal) churchyard. Pass to the right of the church, a most attractive and interesting building which retains an impressive Norman nave and was extensively remodelled in the Georgian period.

Follow the path to the left and bear right to go through two kissing-gates in quick succession. Walk across a field, keeping parallel to a wire fence on the right, go through a gate, and then keep over to the right-hand side of the field alongside a fence.

Go through a metal gate, walk along the right edge of a cricket field and in the corner keep ahead along an enclosed path to a lane **C**.

Turn right, cross the River Kennet, then follow the narrow lane around right-and left-hand bends and head up to a T-junction. Turn left and at a fork ahead, take the right-hand, tarmac drive **D**. After passing in front of a bungalow, the drive becomes a rough track which heads uphill through trees. Cross a track, continue up to cross another and take the narrow, tree-lined path ahead (Cock-a-troop Lane) – this

Savernake Forest

may be overgrown in places – then enter Savernake Forest.

Originally a royal forest, in the 16th century Savernake passed into the ownership of the powerful Seymour family – it was here that Henry VIII courted his third wife, Jane Seymour – and at the end of the 17th century passed to the Bruces, later earls of Ailesbury. It is still owned by that family, but most of it is leased to the Forestry Commission. Savernake is noted for its avenues, particularly the Grand Avenue, a great beech-lined drive planted by the third Earl of Ailesbury in the 18th century.

Keep ahead to a public footpath sign and turn left along a track **E**. Pass beside a barrier and continue through a beautiful stretch of woodland, descending slightly to a lane. Turn right along it to the A4, turn right and after a few yards turn sharp left **F** along a straight forest track. Go down the slope, pass a circular parking-and-turning area on the right under some beech trees and after about 30 yds, veer half right at a barrier, following a straight track up a gentle slope. Pass through extensive woodland to reach fields bordering the track. Continue ahead to a barrier beyond which is the junction for Eight Walks. Take the second right exit **G** (no through road – 20mph limit) and where it bends left after nearly a mile, keep ahead beside a barrier along a rough track. About 100 yds before reaching a road, turn right **H** on to a clear woodland path (Church Walk) which gently descends. Keep right at a fork to reach an open grass area beyond the trees. At a fork continue along the left-hand path, heading gently uphill across grass to re-enter trees. Keep ahead on a broad grassy path, continue ahead at the first crossroads and descend to a junction with a track. Here

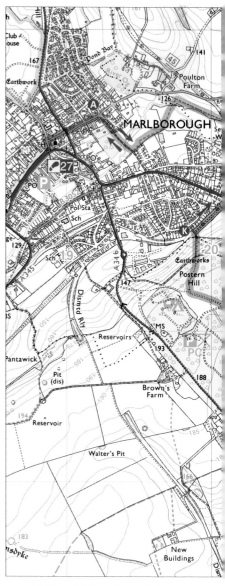

turn left **J** and follow the track (Long Harry) through the trees, eventually reaching a track and then a barrier immediately beyond it. Continue to Postern Hill picnic site and when the track bends left (just beyond a sign Barbecue Hearth – bookable area), take the right-hand fork. Pass a sign 'Site 6' and then bend right at the next junction. Keep along the right edge of an open area of grassland, follow it

round to the right by a sign for Site 3 and follow the broad path through trees. Cross over a path and descend with views of Marlborough to reach the former Chiseldon and Marlborough railway, now a designated walking and cycling route. Turn right **K**.

Walk along the hedge-lined track which, after passing under a bridge, curves gradually left. The next section is beautifully tree-lined and there is a

dramatic view as you cross a bridge high above the River Kennet. Continue through woodland and look out for wooden rails and steps on both sides of the track. Here turn left **B** down the steps, rejoining the outward route, and retrace your steps into Marlborough and the starting point of the walk. ●

Burrington Combe, Dolebury Warren and Black Down

Burrington Combe, Dolebury Warren and Black Down

		GPS waypoints
Start	Burrington Combe	🖊 ST 476 588
Distance	9¼ miles (14.9km) Shorter version 6½ miles (10.5km)	**A** ST 476 590 **B** ST 465 588
Height gain	Longer route 1,380 feet (420m) Shorter route 790 feet (240m)	**C** ST 450 594 **D** ST 446 590
Approximate time	5 hours (3½ hours for shorter walk)	**E** ST 465 586
Parking	Burrington Combe car park (free) opposite the Rock of Ages and above the Burrington pub	**F** ST 467 574 **G** ST 478 571 **H** ST 490 577
Route terrain	Woodland tracks, open grassland, heather moorland; several steep and lengthy ascents	**J** ST 473 583
Dog friendly	Dogs to be kept under control at all times; on lead in Mendip Lodge Wood	
Ordnance Survey maps	Landranger 182 (Weston-super-Mare), Explorer 141 (Cheddar Gorge & Mendip Hills West)	

This walk takes you to the highest point of the Mendips at Black Down, and as a result there are some fairly strenuous climbs. Most of the route is through lovely woods and across open heathland, with superb views over the Mendips and, from the higher points, across to the Bristol Channel coast. The shorter version omits the National Trust area of Dolebury Warren, one of the fine viewpoints.

Burrington Combe is a deep ravine in the Mendips, almost as dramatic as the better known Cheddar Gorge to the south. Opposite the car park is the Rock of Ages, so called because a local 18th-century clergyman, Augustus Toplady, is supposed to have composed the hymn of that name while sheltering from a storm in a cleft in the rock. It is difficult to see how it could provide much shelter today.

🖊 From the car park turn right along the road, passing the **Burrington**

Inn. Cross the road opposite the bus stop and bear left along a track (not the lane, a little farther on). In front of the first house (left), look carefully for an enclosed path with a metal handrail, and turn left along it **A**. This steeply ascending path runs through trees to a narrow lane. Turn left; at a public footpath sign turn right on to a path, to enter Mendip Lodge Wood, soon bearing left then right uphill – the track later flattens out.

After about ¾ mile pass a large

Climbers above the car park in Burrington Combe

ruined building on the left. About 50 yds later, bear left along an uphill track and at a footpath post turn right down to a waymarked stile. Climb it, turn left and continue along an uphill, enclosed track under an avenue of trees as far as a waymarked stile on the right by a Woodland Trust notice **B**.

Here the shorter walk keeps ahead, rejoining the full walk at point **E***.*

For the full walk climb the stile and continue along a path that initially keeps along the left inside edge of the woodland. Later head downhill along a winding track through the trees; follow this to its end. Turn left over a stile, with a house above left. Bear right through a signed kissing-gate and follow the path into and through woodland. Eventually the corner of the wood is reached, with a stile ahead.

Do not cross the stile but turn left uphill **C** along the right inside edge of the wood, cross one track and continue steadily uphill to a second. Cross that and bear slightly right to follow the main winding, uphill path through thick woodland to a stile. Climb it, keep ahead through gorse and scrub to a waymark post, and turn right along a clear path, soon passing through a gate, then heading downhill. At a path junction, turn left uphill through a gate **D**. The track first curves left, then bears right and continues across the extensive earthworks of a large Iron Age fort. After passing through the outer ramparts, continue along a lovely, grassy ridge path, from which there are grand views on both sides, to a stile. Climb it, keep ahead through trees. As you emerge from the trees look for a Limestone Link post on the left. Bear right and head downhill, curving left to another stile. Climb that and follow a grassy track across a field, by an intermittent line of trees on the right. Climb another stile, here leaving Dolebury Warren, to reach a T-junction and turn right **E**, here rejoining the shorter route.

Follow a track through woodland, keep ahead at a crossroads of tracks and bear right to meet another track. Bear left, passing a Forestry Commission

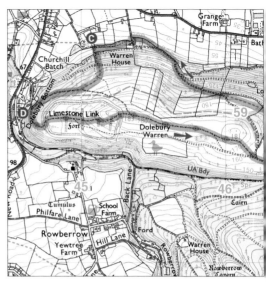

Rowberrow Warren sign (left), along a broad, steadily ascending track towards Black Down. Keep ahead uphill all the while, and at the next signed crossroads turn left **F**, soon emerging from the trees through a gate on to the open heathland of Black Down.

Keep ahead across the down, crossing one track, and on reaching the second path junction bear left on a narrow, sandy path **G**. After 500 yds bear left off the narrow track onto a grassy path. The path passes to the left of the triangulation pillar at Beacon Batch, at 1,067 ft the highest point on the Mendips. Although it is not on a right of way, the Conservators who manage this area of common land have no objection to walkers making the brief diversion to the right in order to enjoy the magnificent view, provided that you keep to an obvious path. In clear weather the spectacular, panoramic view extends across the Mendips, the Somerset Levels and coast to the Quantocks and the hills of South Wales on the horizon.

Retrace your steps to the grassy path,

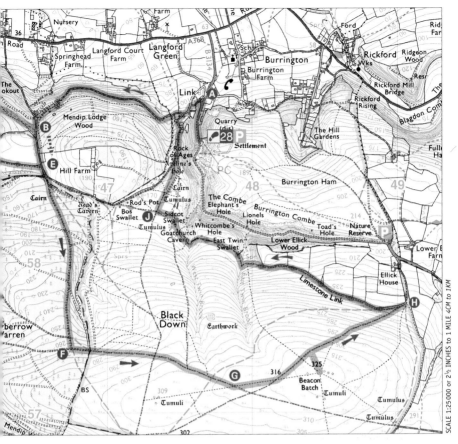

and turn right. Continue downhill to approach a junction of tracks and paths by a tall footpath post; just before the post turn sharp left **H**. At a fork a few yards ahead take the right-hand path to continue along the bottom edge of Black Down. Soon Burrington Combe can be seen over to the right. Descend into trees, follow the path right to ford a brook and later descend to ford another one. Follow the path eventually to meet a clear crossroads of tracks and paths **J**.

Turn right and follow the track downhill to meet another under trees.

Turn right downhill, soon passing a cottage (left). Continue downhill through woodland and at a 'Road Used as a Public Path' sign, turn right again and retrace your steps to the start. ●

Dolebury Warren

Further Information

 ## Walking Safety

Although the reasonably gentle countryside that is the subject of this book offers no real dangers to walkers at any time of the year, it is still advisable to take sensible precautions and follow certain well-tried guidelines.

Always take with you both warm and waterproof clothing and sufficient food and drink. Wear suitable footwear, such as strong walking-boots or shoes that give a good grip over stony ground, on slippery slopes and in muddy conditions. Try to obtain a local weather forecast and bear it in mind before you start. Do not be afraid to abandon your proposed route and return to your starting point in the event of a sudden and unexpected deterioration in the weather.

All the walks described in this book will be safe to do, given due care and respect, even during the winter. Indeed, a crisp, fine winter day often provides perfect walking conditions, with firm ground underfoot and a clarity that is not possible to achieve at any other time of the year.

The most difficult hazard likely to be encountered is mud, especially when walking along woodland and field paths, farm tracks and bridleways – the latter in particular can often get churned up by cyclists and horses. In summer, an additional difficulty may be narrow and overgrown paths, particularly along the edges of cultivated fields. Neither should constitute a major problem provided that the appropriate footwear is worn.

 ## Walkers and the Law

The Countryside and Rights of Way Act (CRoW Act 2000) extends the rights of access previously enjoyed by walkers in England and Wales. Implementation of these rights began on 19 September 2004. The Act amends existing legislation and for the first time provides access on foot to certain types of land – defined as mountain, moor, heath, down and registered common land.

Where You Can Go
Rights of Way
Prior to the introduction of the CRoW Act, walkers could only legally access the countryside along public rights of way. These are either 'footpaths' (for walkers only) or 'bridleways' (for walkers, riders on horseback and pedal cyclists). A third category called 'Byways open to all traffic' (BOATs), is used by motorised vehicles as well as those using non-mechanised transport. Mainly they are green lanes, farm and estate roads, although occasionally they will be found crossing mountainous area.

Rights of way are marked on Ordnance Survey maps. Look for the green broken lines on the Explorer maps, or the red dashed lines on Landranger maps.

The term 'right of way' means exactly what it says. It gives a right of passage over what, for the most part, is private land. Under pre-CRoW legislation walkers were required to keep to the line of the right of way and not stray onto land on either side. If you did inadvertently wander off the right of way, either because of faulty map reading or because the route was not clearly indicated on the ground, you were technically trespassing.

Local authorities have a legal obligation to ensure that rights of way are kept clear and free of obstruction, and are signposted where they leave metalled roads. The duty of local authorities to install signposts extends to the placing of signs along a path or way, but only where the authority considers it necessary to have a signpost or waymark to assist persons unfamiliar with the locality.

The New Access Rights
Access Land
As well as being able to walk on existing

Countryside Access Charter

Your rights of way are:

- public footpaths – on foot only. Sometimes waymarked in yellow
- bridle-ways – on foot, horseback and pedal cycle. Sometimes waymarked in blue
- byways (usually old roads), most 'roads used as public paths' and, of course, public roads – all traffic has the right of way

Use maps, signs and waymarks to check rights of way. Ordnance Survey Explorer and Landranger maps show most public rights of way

On rights of way you can:

- take a pram, pushchair or wheelchair if practicable
- take a dog (on a lead or under close control)
- take a short route round an illegal obstruction or remove it sufficiently to get past

You have a right to go for recreation to:

- public parks and open spaces – on foot
- most commons near older towns and cities – on foot and sometimes on horseback
- private land where the owner has a formal agreement with the local authority

In addition you can use the following by local or established custom or consent, but ask for advice if you are unsure:

- many areas of open country, such as moorland, fell and coastal areas, especially those in the care of the National Trust, and some commons
- some woods and forests, especially those owned by the Forestry Commission
- country parks and picnic sites
- most beaches
- canal towpaths
- some private paths and tracks Consent sometimes extends to horse-riding and cycling

For your information:

- county councils and London boroughs maintain and record rights of way, and register commons
- obstructions, dangerous animals, harassment and misleading signs on rights of way are illegal and you should report them to the county council
- paths across fields can be ploughed, but must normally be reinstated within two weeks
- landowners can require you to leave land to which you have no right of access
- motor vehicles are normally permitted only on roads, byways and some 'roads used as public paths'

Further Information

rights of way, under the new legislation you now have access to large areas of open land. You can of course continue to use rights of way footpaths to cross this land, but the main difference is that you can now lawfully leave the path and wander at will, but only in areas designated as access land.

Where to Walk
Areas now covered by the new access rights – Access Land – are shown on Ordnance Survey Explorer maps bearing the access land symbol on the front cover.

'Access Land' is shown on Ordnance Survey maps by a light yellow tint surrounded by a pale orange border. New orange coloured 'i' symbols on the maps will show the location

of permanent access information boards installed by the access authorities.

Restrictions
The right to walk on access land may lawfully be restricted by landowners. Landowners can, for any reason, restrict access for up to 28 days in any year. They cannot however close the land:
- on bank holidays;
- for more than four Saturdays and Sundays in a year;
- on any Saturday from 1 June to 11 August; or
- on any Sunday from 1 June to the end of September.

They have to provide local authorities with

five working days' notice before the date of closure unless the land involved is an area of less than five hectares or the closure is for less than four hours. In these cases landowners only need to provide two hours' notice.

Whatever restrictions are put into place on access land they have no effect on existing rights of way, and you can continue to walk on them.

Dogs

Dogs can be taken on access land, but must be kept on leads of two metres or less between 1 March and 31 July, and at all times where they are near livestock. In addition landowners may impose a ban on all dogs from fields where lambing takes place for up to six weeks in any year. Dogs may be banned from moorland used for grouse shooting and breeding for up to five years.

In the main, walkers following the routes in this book will continue to follow existing rights of way, but a knowledge and understanding of the law as it affects walkers, plus the ability to distinguish access land marked on the maps, will enable anyone who wishes to depart from paths that cross access land either to take a shortcut, to enjoy a view or to explore.

General Obstructions

Obstructions can sometimes cause a problem on a walk and the most common of these is where the path across a field has been ploughed over. It is legal for a farmer to plough up a path provided that it is restored within two weeks. This does not always happen and you are faced with the dilemma of following the line of the path, even if this means treading on crops, or walking round the edge of the field. Although the later course of action seems the most sensible, it does mean that you would be trespassing.

Other obstructions can vary from overhanging vegetation to wire fences across the path, locked gates or even a cattle feeder on the path.

Use common sense. If you can get round the obstruction without causing damage, do so. Otherwise only remove as much of the obstruction as is necessary to secure passage.

If the right of way is blocked and cannot be followed, there is a long-standing view that in such circumstances there is a right to deviate, but this cannot wholly be relied on. Although it is accepted in law that highways (and that includes rights of way) are for the public service, and if the usual track is impassable, it is for the general good that people should be entitled to pass into another line. However, this should not be taken as indicating a right to deviate whenever a way becomes impassable. If in doubt, retreat.

Report obstructions to the local authority and/or The Ramblers.

 Useful Organisations

Campaign to Protect Rural England
128 Southwark Street, London SE1 0SW
Tel. 020 7981 2800
www.cpre.org.uk

English Heritage
Customer Services, PO Box 569, Swindon SN2 2YP
Tel. 0870 3331181
www.english-heritage.org.uk

Forestry Commission
Bank House, Bank Street, Coleford, Gloucestershire GL16 8BA
Tel. 01594 833057
www.forestry.gov.uk

National Trust
Membership and general enquiries
PO Box 39, Warrington WA5 7WD
Tel. 0870 458 4000
www.nationaltrust.org.uk

Natural England
John Dower House, Crescent Place, Cheltenham GL50 3RA

Tel. 0300 060 2481
www.naturalengland.org.uk

Ordnance Survey
Romsey Road, Maybush, Southampton
SO16 4GU
Tel. 08456 05 05 05 (Lo-call)
www.ordnancesurvey.co.uk

Ramblers' Association
2nd Floor, Camelford House, 87-90 Albert
Embankment, London SE1 7TW
Tel. 0207 339 8500
www.ramblers.org.uk

Somerset Visitor Centre
Sedgemoor Services, M5 South,
Axbridge (closed Sat. and Sun. in winter)
Tel. 01934 750833

Local tourist information offices:
Amesbury: 01980 622833
Avebury: 01672 539179
Bradford on Avon: 01225 865797
Bridgwater: 01278 436438
Burnham-on-Sea: 01278 787852
Cartgate: 01935 829333
Chard: 01460 65710
Cheddar: 01934 744071
Chippenham: 01249 665970
Corsham: 01249 714660
Devizes: 01380 729408
Frome: 01373 467271
Glastonbury: 01458 832954
Malmesbury: 01666 823748
Marlborough: 01672 512663
Melksham: 01225 707424
Mere: 01747 861211
Minehead: 01643 702624
Salisbury: 01722 334956
Shepton Mallet: 01749 345258
Street: 01458 447384
Swindon: 01793 530328/466454
Taunton: 01823 336344
Trowbridge: 01225 710535
Warminster: 01985 218548
Wellington: 01823 663379
Wells: 01749 672552
Weston-super-Mare: 01934 888800
Yeovil: 01935 845946

Youth Hostels Association
Trevelyan House, Dimple Road, Matlock,
Derbyshire DE4 3YH
Tel. 01629 592600
www.yha.org.uk
Traveline: 0871 200 2233
National train enquiry line: 0845 484950

 Ordnance Survey maps of Somerset, the Mendips and Wiltshire

Somerset, the Mendips and Wiltshire are covered by Ordnance Survey 1:50 000 (1 ¼ inches to 1 mile or 2cm to 1km) scale Landranger map sheets 172, 173, 174, 181, 182, 183, 184, 193, 194 and 195. These all-purpose maps are packed with useful information compiled to help you explore the area. In addition, they show viewpoints, picnic sites, places of interest and caravan and camping sites, as well as other information likely to be of interest.

To examine the Somerset, Wiltshire and Mendips area in more detail, and especially if you are planning walks, we recommend the following Ordnance Survey Explorer maps at 1:25 000 (2½ inches to 1 mile or 4cm to 1km) scale:

118 (Shaftesbury & Cranborne Chase)
128 (Taunton & Blackdown Hills)
129 (Yeovil & Sherborne)
130 (Salisbury & Stonehenge)
141 (Cheddar Gorge & Mendip Hills West)
142 (Shepton Mallet & Mendip Hills East)
143 (Warminster & Trowbridge)
153 (Weston-super-Mare & Bleadon Hill)
154 (Bristol West & Portishead)
156 (Chippenham & Bradford-on-Avon)
157 (Marlborough & Savernake Forest)
158 (Newbury & Hungerford)
170 (Abingdon, Wantage & Vale of White Horse)

To get to the area, use the Ordnance Survey OS Travel Map-Route Great Britain at 1:625 000 scale (1 inch to 10 miles or 4cm to 25 km).

Ordnance Survey maps and guides are available from most booksellers, stationers and newsagents.

crimsonPUBLISHING

Easy to navigate... informative and packed with practical information
Which? Holiday

Unearth...

The best of Britain series

ACCESSIBLE, CONTEMPORARY GUIDES BY LOCAL EXPERTS

ISBN: 978 1 85458 424 3

ISBN: 978 1 85458 463 2

ISBN: 978 1 85458 426 7

ISBN: 978 1 85458 423 6

ISBN: 978 1 85458 422 9

ISBN: 978 1 85458 425 0

AVAILABLE NOW

Edinburgh: 978 1 85458 464 9
Northern Ireland: 978 1 85458 465 6
The Peak District: 978 1 85458 467 0

Buy your guide at **www.crimsonpublishing.co.uk**